ANCIENT VOICES,
CURRENT AFFAIRS

relationship with all beings and to the significance of cooperative action.

Bioresonance is a word that signifies patterns, the drumbeat of the Earth and our own interaction with that drumbeat. In healthy systems, our brains, our breath, and the timbre of our voices resonate harmonically with the drumming heartbeat, the pulse of the Earth. As the Earth's pulse is quickened by an influx of energy from the center of the universe, we find those patterns that have created discord or blocks in the pulsing flow initially appear more chaotic as they seek resolution. Yet with the release of energy potential that was occluded, abundant opportunity arises for growth and realization.

There is a phrase that is used among many of our elders these days: "Remember the original instructions." These original instructions are the patterns encoded within the DNA helix. Just as a guitar being tuned in one part of a room sets the strings of a piano in another part of the room to moving, so does the tuning of the universe set our minds in motion. Patterns of suffering have been seeded by the dissonance between what is ideal and what *is*. The movement toward the ideal—including the hopes of all beings—creates pathways of resolution. Within the discord, with careful direction the resolution is revealed.

Just as within the curve of an ocean wave there is turbulence and wind, the winds of change are moving throughout all beings. The pulses and the waves are stirred by this fine-tuning process. Within the curve of that wave resides great turbulence, which is also energy potential, so that we as human beings can bring forth that encoded potential of health and right relationship to fruition.

Considering the waves of change as being an opportunity, we human beings now have the option to re-create our relationships, to participate in the manifestation of community, government, high art, and service. As this potential becomes more apparent, we see that certain pathways exist through which the forms arise. The first pathway is that of clear intention—that we hold the intention to be in right relationships with our families, our friends, our co-workers, the nations, and the land. Nations are indeed a living organism affecting and affected by the environment in which they live.

⟪⟪⟨INVOCATION⟩⟫⟫

*W*e stand today on the threshold of a dream, a harvesting of sacred seeds. May Steven McFadden's *Ancient Voices, Current Affairs* reveal to all the present opportunity to transform discord and cultivate the seeds of right relationship.

As nature has its seasonal cycles, so are there also cycles of planetary growth and dissolution. With the reunification of East and West Germany and the breaking up of the Soviet Union we have seen the opportunity for the illusions that separate people to fall away. This is a most exciting time as these illusions fall away, and it requires diligence on the part of every human being: diligence in cultivating thoughts and actions that are indeed beneficial.

When we consider the myth of the Rainbow Warrior, we see that the rainbow is a bridge that connects all cultures and that the greatest warriors only war upon ignorance—their own as well as that of others—by changing the thought patterns of discord and revealing methods of resolution. In these years leading to the year 2003, every human being will feel the deep influence of unconscious patterns rising to the surface of the mind, which are then acted out in national and international activities. What arises is a recognition of that which has kept humans separate from the Earth and from one another.

A tone arises as a pulse from the Earth, the sun, and the center of our Milky Way galaxy. Paying attention to this pulse, or heartbeat, enables us to come again into resonant harmony with the pulse of the Earth and one another. Our personal thoughts and actions contribute to the future a fourth note, which creates a chord and is perceived as a field of action. We were taught this is called the Age of Flowers, when the minds of the people return to the understanding of our

⟨⟨⟨⟨ ACKNOWLEDGMENTS ⟩⟩⟩⟩

Many friends and acquaintances have made this book possible by contributing inspiration, support, and teachings. Among the many helpers are my loving wife, Carolyn; Lane Masterson; Mark Lerner; José Argüelles; Medicine Story; Marcia Starck; Satyena Ananda; Jonathan and Karen Goldman; Kelley Hunter; Helyn Connerr; Tomiki; Corinne McLaughlin; Gordon Davidson; Tom Cratsley; Kathie Gabriel; the Watkinson family; John Harvey Gray; Linda Aranda; John S. Mercer; Carol Dubois; Carolyn Worrell; Paula Cercel; Becky Mulkern; Bryan Field; Betsey Browne; Pauline Zimmer; Brooke Medicine Eagle; Arthur and Marilyn Perkins; Bob and Celeste Longacre; Dhyani Ywahoo; Jeff Bumbaco; Linda Lindgren; Sig Longren; Oh Shinnah; Ross Jennings; Rosemary Cathcart; Dorsey Toney; Shabri Red Bird; Juan Gonzalez; Scott Guynup and Page Bryant; Brant Secunda; Nicki Scully; Nick Michael; John and Charla Tarwater; Bill, Debbie, and Noah Joiner; and many others I have surely neglected to mention.

For career inspiration, I thank my uncle, Paul Fitzsimmons. For technical and creative excellence and for overall support, I thank the entire staff of Bear & Company, especially Barbara and Gerry Clow for their vision, Gail Vivino for her careful and critical editing, Amy Frost for her clarity, Barbara Doern Drew for her supervision, and Angela Werneke and Marilyn Hager Biethan for their artistic vision.

I offer my thanks and deep appreciation to the elders, living and in spirit, who gave voice to the visions that are the basis of this book.

⟨⟨⟨⟨ ILLUSTRATIONS ⟩⟩⟩⟩

FIGURES

PHOTOS

⟪⟨⟨ CONTENTS ⟩⟩⟩

With love to
Carolyn Mercer-McFadden, Ph.D.:
Woman with Many Fires.
And for All Our Relations,
especially our godchildren.

LIBRARY OF CONGRESS CATALOGING-IN-PUBLICATION DATA

McFadden, Steven S. H., 1948-
    Ancient voices, current affairs : the legend of the rainbow warriors / by
Steven McFadden ; invocation by Dhyani Ywahoo.
        p.   cm.
    Includes bibliographical references.
    ISBN 1-879181-00-2
    1. New Age movement. 2. Civilization, Modern—1950- 3. Human
ecology—Religious aspects. 4. Indians of North America—Religion and
mythology—Miscellanea. 5. Indigenous peoples—Miscellanea. 6. Mythology—Miscellanea. I. Title. II. Title: Rainbow warriors.
BP605.N48M373 1992
291.1'78362—dc20   92-8542
                                                                                  CIP

ANCIENT VOICES

CURRENT AFFAIRS

THE LEGEND OF THE RAINBOW WARRIORS

STEVEN McFADDEN

INVOCATION BY DHYANI YWAHOO

BEAR & COMPANY

PUBLISHING

SANTA FE, NEW MEXICO

Just as an infant recognizes its parents and parents recognize the needs of their child, that innate ability of subtle communication reawakening is a path of human survival. When we consider how parents recognize when their child is in need and come to the rescue, we can see a similar dynamic with groups and the environment. This dynamic has the potential to purify the waters and the winds. For example, just as energy holds an electron in a neutron's orbit, so do similar fields hold us in relationship to the Earth, to the community, and to one another, and the basic resonance or first tone is that of our families. I interpret my elders' counsel to remember the original instructions as being about reawakening those resonant fields of communication that enable us to work in a synergistic way with our families, our friends, our co-workers, our nations, and the very living planet herself.

These original instructions are beyond dogma. They are like the cords wrapped around a thread that make the fabric strong or the overtones of a melody that give a symphony its cohesiveness. It is no longer a matter of leaders leading us. Rather, we must lead ourselves into right relationships with each other and with the Earth. This will require our cooperative interaction, clear visioning, recognition of the relationships, and developing the skills of reconciliation. The process of healing begins in our own hearts as we consider what it is that we wish to accomplish, how it will benefit our relatives and the future generations, and who we will invite to build it with us. The great lesson that humanity is now receiving is the lesson of right relationship. We can no longer relinquish our responsibility if, indeed, we already have, and it is no longer possible or wise for a few leaders to make decisions for many. We must all participate in this form arising.

Consider time as moving energy, like the sand in the hourglass; the past, present and future now fold upon each other, enabling humankind to correct the errors of the past and extract from the collective experience the lessons learned. The millennium is upon us in the form of quickened radiation from the stars, an inpouring of energy through the holes in the ozone layer and holes in time, revealing the inconsistency of a worldview that gives humanity the right to dominate the environment and that sees people as being incongruent with the fields of life. We have learned that the oceans are affected by that which we attempt to cast away, decimating life in the seas. Energy is neither lost nor created. We share in the dance of change; the winds are formed by what we cast aloft. The actions of individuals and nations bear directly upon the present and future.

All beings living on Earth have something to contribute to her well-being, and governments, including their citizenry, aid the cycle of reciprocity. The ideal of a millennium of peace is within our means. Such technology is now available to invite direct participation of citizens in decision making and planning. Let us remember that we are children of the same mother. While the archetypes of her action are colored by culture and environment, all particulars resolve into the one truth: we are living on Earth.

The garden of Eden, the realm of Ongawi, the perfect ideal is revealed by the gardener's skill in planting seeds of right relationship. The great peace begins as a seed in our hearts. The dream stirs us all to consider our actions unto future generations. The "how" is revealed in our hoping. Envision, energize with prayerful appreciation; invite all those who have marveled at the beauty of the rainbow to build cooperatively the world of beauty. All the gifts of heaven have long been engraved in our hearts, and now is the time to sweep away confusion and take note of what is.

Ven. Dhyani Ywahoo
May 1992
Bristol, Vermont

Dhyani Ywahoo is the founder and spiritual director of the Sunray Meditation Society in Bristol, Vermont.

⟨⟨⟨PROLOGUE⟩⟩⟩

Throughout the inhabited world, in all times and under every circumstance, the myths of man have flourished; and they have been the living inspiration of whatever else may have appeared out of the activities of the human body and mind. . . . Myth is the secret opening through which the inexhaustible energies of the cosmos pour into human cultural manifestation.
—Joseph Campbell

*F*or most of the twentieth century, the dominant myth in the United States has been a version of the American Dream suggesting that most people can attain great wealth and that happiness will follow. However, the promised wealth has never been attainable for millions, people who now live on the streets or in substandard housing. Those who have attained the wealth, by and large, may now realize that this part of the dream is hollow. Material riches in and of themselves bring no peace, carry no happiness. Tragically, the unbridled pursuit of this dream, often by people deep in sleep, has plunged us into a nightmare of environmental devastation, ethical bankruptcy, and cultural confusion.

Perhaps more passionately than our ancestors, we yearn for a dream that can unify us and direct us again in a good way. We seem to have lost it all: our tribe, our extended families, and our geographic, linguistic, and cultural roots. Where are we in this New World we call America? What have we made of our lives together?

For the most part, we live in a high-speed, high-tech, electronically stimulated world of abstraction. The threat of nuclear or environmental annihilation hangs over each moment. While there is material wealth for some, there is spiritual poverty for most. In a sense, all this is the result of myth gone awry. Is it any wonder that we are rejecting the old myths?

As we cast about for meaning and direction, two venerable and related myths have steadily begun to emerge: the myth of a New Age and the Legend of the Rainbow Warriors. Though widely disparaged, the myth of a New Age echoes an ancient theme in storytelling: paradise lost, paradise regained. We have lost paradise in our modern world. Is it therefore surprising that there should arise in our epoch many hopeful myths of a New Age, a time when paradise will be regained?

As we approach the millennium, many storytellers are animating these emerging myths with their words, their art, and their music. Rainbows are steadily firing the imaginations of many millions of people. But will these myths penetrate world culture sufficiently to make a difference? That is a question only historians will be able to answer.

This book seeks to further clarify the emerging myth of the rainbow and to demonstrate its living connection to the news unfolding each night on the television screen. The technique for telling this story is a blend of journalism and mythic storytelling. Through journalism, I have gathered critical news stories and sought to establish how seemingly unrelated events can have a deep connection. Through myth, I have taken the process a step further and offered an explanation, or meaning, for the events—thereby linking ancient voices with current affairs. This technique might well be called mythojournalism.

The various stories in this book are, in fact, one. Together they tell a saga that is larger than the sum of their collective parts. The thread that links them is the Legend of the Rainbow Warriors, part of the emerging myth of a New Age. In brief, the Legend of the Rainbow Warriors says that when the Earth becomes desperately sick through the doings of human beings, some of the people will recognize that they are steadily destroying themselves and their Earth Mother. With spiritual support, the Rainbow Warriors—people of all colors and faiths—will come to the rescue, eventually establishing a long and joyous reign of peace.

This modern myth suggests there will be no one hero in this time, no George Washington or Joan of Arc to rescue us from the great dilemma we have created. We must do it ourselves. In that sense, the Legend of the Rainbow Warriors is, to use a modern term, a holistic myth, wherein we all have both the opportunity and the responsibility to become spiritually awakened heroes.

The overall myth points out the general direction that we need to travel: a direction in which there is full respect for the self, for others, and for all the creations who share life upon the planet. By proceeding in this direction, we will create a spiritually informed culture that uses scientific technology to maintain freedom and enhance the balance of life. From that perspective, this book is a journalist's dispatch on how the myth of a New Age is unfolding in the world.

The news events that are reported within the context of the rainbow prophecies are all true. You can flip open *Facts on File* and verify them; they are the stuff of daily news stories from *The New York Times*, *The Boston Globe*, CBS, and other standard sources. Does this mean that the legends and prophecies are true? Who can say with certainty? I know only that people need myth in their lives and that, as myth, the rainbow legends have inspired me and helped give meaning to the chaos of the times. I have also seen how the stories inspire and uplift others when I share them in gatherings both large and small. This gives me hope.

For these many reasons, I offer this collection: to clarify the myth, to show its connection to present reality, and to inspire people to work toward making the dream real by engaging in an ancient quest—seeking practical ways to bring heaven to Earth.

As Joseph Campbell has suggested, ultimately it matters little whether a myth is based on ascertainable fact or not. What matters is whether the myth helps people to live better, more satisfying lives—not just for themselves, but as part of a community, as part of the fabric of life on this planet. In this way, if people choose it out of their intelligence and free will, a myth that has been unreal can become real.

ONE

The Legend
of the Rainbow Warriors

*I*n the spring of 1983, I met a handsome young woman named Brooke Medicine Eagle. She was standing in a circle of people on a wooded knoll near the Hudson River, and she was striking a drum rhythmically to match the silent but all-pervading heartbeat of the Earth Mother. She asked all of the people in the circle to acknowledge the heartbeat of the Earth as their own, and then she told the story of her vision.

Brooke is a woman of Crow and Sioux heritage. As she stood on the knoll, she told how, in preparation for her work as a healer, she had purified herself in a sweatlodge and then climbed to the summit of Bear Butte in South Dakota to fast for four days and nights, crying out to the Great Mystery for a vision to guide her.

In time, as the moon began to rise and a rainbow filled half the twilit sky, her vision unfolded. A holy woman dressed in buckskin appeared and stood next to her. As moonbeams shone upon the woman, Brooke saw that each atom of her buckskin was a rainbow, every particle reflecting the full sparkling spectrum.

Then, as a double circle of friends and teachers danced about both of them in a simple sacred way, the Rainbow Woman began to feed energy to Brooke through her solar plexus. Some of that energy Brooke sensed physically, some emotionally, some intellectually.

Much of what was communicated to her, Brooke later said, she did not fully understand. But she was able to grasp a part of the message, and that is what she shared with us in 1983. She said her vision revealed what is obvious to those who look upon the world with an open heart: that we are living in a time of great change. As a result of human action, much of the world is desperately out of balance. In this time of great change, we can destroy our world or we can heal it. For healing to come about, we need to honor the spirit within ourselves and within all things. We must remember that the Earth is our mother, and we must take care of her.

After telling her vision, Brooke—whose sacred name is Daughter of the Rainbow of the Morning Star Clan Whose Helpers Are the Sun and the Moon and Whose Medicine Is the Eagle—turned to look at the people who encircled her. With her eyes flashing and her voice ringing, she said that for several days after her vision

Photo 1. Brooke Medicine Eagle.

she saw rainbows in the sky, even over the Golden Gate Bridge in San Francisco. During those days she began to understand more of her vision. "We have the opportunity to build a rainbow bridge into a Golden Age," she explained. "But to do this we must do it together with all the colors of the rainbow, with all the peoples, all the beings of the world. We who are alive on Earth today are the Rainbow Warriors who face the challenge of building this bridge."

As I listened to Brooke tell her story, I was entranced. Her powerful presence and dramatic story touched some remote part of me, as if I had heard the story before in childhood or dreamed a dream of rainbows on my own. I wanted to understand more.

In the weeks and months that followed, I set time aside for reading and meditating on the rainbow. I learned that the rainbow theme is sounded frequently in the dreams and visions of the holy men and women of the Native American tradition, and that it is a prominent theme in North American prophecy. In particular, I found a collection of related dreams and visions recorded in a slim volume by William Willoya and Vinson Brown entitled *Warriors of the Rainbow—Strange and Prophetic Dreams of the Indian Peoples.*

From among many versions of the rainbow vision, this book tells the story from the perspective of Eyes of Fire of the Cree nation, Black Elk of the Lakota Sioux, Quetzalcoatl of the Toltec, Plenty Coups of the Crow, Montezuma of the Aztec, The Great Peacemaker of the Iroquois Six Nations, and several others. Though they lived at different times and places, they shared a sense of what was to come.

The Legend

In brief, in amalgamated form, here is the Legend of the Rainbow Warriors as described in ancient days by Native American visionaries, who foresaw the arrival of light-skinned people on Turtle Island (North America):

The light-skinned people will come out of the Eastern sea in great canoes powered by huge white wings, like giant birds. The people who get off these boats will also be like birds, but they will have two different kinds of feet. One of their feet will be like that of a dove, the other like that of an eagle. The foot of the dove will represent a beautiful new religion of love and kindness, and the foot of the eagle will represent strength, technology, and war-making ability. The sharp foot of the eagle will dominate, for though they will talk much of the new religion, not all of the light-skinned people will live by it. Instead, they will claw at the Red Nations with their eagle feet, exploiting and enslaving them.

After offering mixed resistance to this clawing, the Indians will lose their spirit and allow themselves to be herded into small, weak enclaves. This will be the way of their world for many years. Then, in time, the world will become very sick. Because of the unrelenting greed of the new culture, the Earth will be filled with deadly liquids and metals, the air will be rendered foul with smoke and ash, and even the rains—which are intended to cleanse the Earth—will plummet in poison drops. Birds will fall from the sky. Fish will turn belly up in the waters. Forests will begin to die.

When these things begin to happen, the Indian people will be all but helpless. But then Light will come from the East, and the Indians will begin to find their strength, their pride, and their wisdom. So will many of their light-skinned brothers and sisters, who will in fact be the reincarnated souls of the Indians who were enslaved or killed by the settlers. Together, they will teach all the people of the world to have reverence for the Earth Mother, of whose very stuff human beings are made.

Under the symbol of the rainbow, all the races and religions will band together to spread the great wisdom of living in harmony with each other and with all the creations of the world. Those who teach this way will be the Warriors of the Rainbow, but they will do no harm. Using peaceful means, after a great struggle they will bring an end to the destruction and desecration of the Earth. Peace and plenty will then reign through a long and joyous Golden Age.

As I read, I absorbed all of these new ideas with great attention. The story haunted me, gnawed at me, and finally, in combination with other forces on my path, drew me into the forests and then onto a mountain alone, in search of a more complete understanding of this legend and its meaning for our times.

In the forests and on the mountain, I was gifted with insight. I learned the way of the four directions and heard the message of the winged ones, the birds. In deep peace on a northern summit, I saw in sharp relief how modern times and the myth were echoes of each other. I resolved to tell the story.

Months passed. I went with my wife to Provincetown, Massachusetts, to rest by the sea. There, amidst the posters, the bumper stickers, and the people in a Greenpeace gift shop, I had another revelation. I saw and felt how deeply others had been influenced by the rainbow vision.

When the founders of Greenpeace heard the rainbow legend, they were out at sea, already working for earthly sanity in a world gone dizzy grasping for material gain. The rainbow hit them so hard that they named Greenpeace's first and foremost ship *The Rainbow Warrior*. The ship became a focal point for inspiration and action, a vehicle through which human beings could assert themselves on behalf of the Earth Mother.

From this feeling of connection with Greenpeace and the Legend of the Rainbow Warriors, I drew hope, strength, and courage. I walked my own part of the rainbow path for two and a half years while Brooke Medicine Eagle walked in the West, studying the lessons that life drew to her. Then Brooke came East for a week, calling another circle of people together near the murky waters of the Charles River in Massachusetts.

When the people arrived and joined in this circle, Brooke took a moment to find her balance. Then she leaned back and opened herself to the Divine, what she called the Great Mystery. With song and story, she sounded the new tone that she hears being set in the world: a tone of the heart, of healing, and of harmony. We all breathed in balance, and then we sang and danced in a sacred way.

Brooke addressed the circle using a common rhetorical device. "I've got some good news and some bad news," she said. "The good news is that those of us who hear these things and feel them deeply are the Rainbow Warriors. We are here now to take on the challenge

Figure 1. The Author's Vision. *"I came to understand that the rainbow path was growing wider."*

of building a rainbow bridge into a time that works for everyone and everything. The bad news is that we must do it today. The time of waiting is over. The Earth changes have begun, and we are called to heal the world."

When I heard Brooke say these things by the banks of the Charles River, they no longer sent me off into a dreamy void. By that time, I had already been to a craggy summit in the far North to seek another vision. There I had seen a star-filled sky, eight rainbows ringing the eastern horizon, and an eagle on the wing higher overhead than I had ever imagined a creature of flesh and blood might reach. Vision had come to me, along with deeper insight. I had spoken with the rainbow and had come to understand that the rainbow path was growing wider. I had seen that the many brothers and sisters who walked it were growing in strength. On that mountain, my heart had filled with peace. Later, as I stood in a circle with Brooke and twenty-five other brothers and sisters, that peace became a power in the world.

TWO

Counsel of the Elders

*A*s there are many colors in the rainbow, so are there many versions of the rainbow legend on Turtle Island—a large land area ranging from the northlands we know as Canada to the southlands we call Mexico. All versions of the legend sound the themes of respect for the Earth, respect for ourselves and each other, and respect for the plants and animals that make our lives possible.

The legends also sound the theme of unity through diversity. Thomas Banyacya, an elder of the Hopi Nation, has observed that "as Native Americans, we believe the rainbow is a sign from the spirit in all things. It is a sign of the union of all peoples, like one big family. The unity of all humanity—many tribes and peoples—is essential."

The Hopi people have many elaborate stories to tell of the rainbow, of the continent known as Turtle Island, and of the role of native people in offering their ancient guidance to modern culture. Other native groups also share in this understanding. For example, as reported by Vinson Brown in *Voices of Earth and Sky*, around 1871 the great chief of the Oglala Sioux, Crazy Horse, had a powerful vision that clearly sounded the rainbow theme:

> He saw his people being driven into spiritual darkness and poverty while the white people prospered in a material way all around them. But even in the darkest times he saw that the eyes of a few of his people kept the light of dawn and the wisdom of the Earth, which they passed on to some of their grandchildren.

He saw the coming of automobiles and airplanes and twice he saw great darkness and heard screams and explosions when millions died in two great world wars.

But after the second great war passed, he saw a time come when his people began to awaken, not all at once, but a few here and there, and then more and more, and he saw that they were dancing in the beautiful light of the Spirit World under the Sacred Tree even while still on Earth. Then he was amazed to see that dancing under that tree were representatives of all races who had become brothers, and he realized that the world would be made new again and in peace and harmony, not just by his people, but by members of all the races of mankind.

Contemporary native leaders also offer a wealth of insight on the teachings of the rainbow. Together, their insights make the many dimensions of the rainbow shimmer with light, adding depth and richness to the myth. Many of the elders who were subjects for my previous book, *Profiles in Wisdom: Native Elders Speak about the Earth*, offered understandings of the rainbow. In that book, their rainbow teachings were widely dispersed. In this book, so they may be seen plainly, those teachings are consolidated.

Seven Prophets, Seven Fires

Grandfather William Commanda of the Algonquin nation is a wisdom keeper of the North. All his life he has lived on the Manawaki Indian Reserve in the Canadian province of Quebec, where he has been a canoe maker, a hunter, and a forestry worker. Grandfather Commanda is the keeper of the Primstaven, a carved wooden staff given to the Indian people by the Vikings more than a thousand years ago. The carvings on the staff tell the prophecies of the Viking people. In essence, these prophecies assert

Photo 2. Grandfather William Commanda. *Author photo.*

that although different people have different ways of understanding it, there is only one Creator, and all people, no matter their color or their religious traditions, come from this Creator. Some day, the carvings on the stick declare, all people will recognize and honor this simple truth.

In addition to the Primstaven, Grandfather Commanda is keeper of the Seven Fires wampum belt, which was fashioned from sea shells in the fifteenth century. Using diamond-shaped symbols, this artifact tells how seven prophets came before the Algonquin people many years ago. They spoke of seven epochs of history, called the Seven Fires. In the Fourth Fire, the prophets said, a light-skinned people would come to the home of the Red Nations, known as Turtle Island, and things would change.

"If the light-skinned race comes in brotherhood and without weapons," the prophets declared, "then there will come a time of wonderful change for generations." But they counseled that if the light-skinned race came wearing the face of death, then the people would have to be careful. The face of brotherhood and the face of death would look similar, but the face of death would soon be revealed in the form of greed for the riches of the land. "You shall know that they wear the face of death," the prophets said, "if the rivers run with poison and the fish become unfit to eat."

The markings on the wampum belt tell a gloom-filled story of greed, environmental destruction, and native suffering.

According to Grandfather Commanda, "It is said that, in the confusing times of the Sixth Fire, a group of visionaries came among the people. They gathered all the priests of the Midewiwin Lodge and told them that the Midewiwin Way was in danger of being destroyed. They gathered all the sacred bundles. They gathered all the scrolls that recorded the ceremonies. All these things were placed in a hollowed-out log from an ironwood tree. Men were lowered over a cliff by long ropes. They dug a hole in the cliff and buried the log where no one would find it. Thus, the teachings of the elders were hidden out of sight, but not out of memory. It was said that when the time came that the Indian People could practice their religion without fear, a little boy would dream where the ironwood log, full of sacred bundles and scrolls, was buried. He would lead his people to that place."

The Seventh Fire on the belt symbolizes hope. As Grandfather Commanda explains, the seventh prophet said that in the time of the Seventh Fire a new people would emerge. They would retrace their steps to find the wisdom that was left by the side of the trail long ago. Their steps would take them to the elders, who they would ask to guide them on their journey. "If the new people remain strong in their quest, the sacred drum will again sound its voice. There will be an awakening of the people, and the Sacred Fire will again be lit. At this time, the light-skinned race will be given a choice between two roads." One road is the road of greed and technology without wisdom or respect for life. This road represents a rush to destruction. The other road is spirituality, a slower path that includes respect for all living things. If we choose the spiritual path, we can light yet another fire, an Eighth Fire, and begin an extended period of peace and healthy growth.

Grandfather Commanda firmly believes that we are now in the time of the Seventh Fire and that the choice of the two roads is before us. He prays every day that we will honor the North and make our choice from the place of wisdom, recognizing Light in all the rainbow creations of the world.

The Return of the Rainbow People

Sun Bear was a Chippewa teacher who traveled the world to share the prophecies of native peoples and to warn of Earth changes. He died June 19, 1992, in Spokane, Washington. The originator of the popular Medicine Wheel Gatherings, Sun Bear spoke with force and eloquence. "All the prophecies of the native people," he said, "speak of a time when the human beings will face a choice between going on the same way with greed and technology or going toward spirit. I feel, and many others feel, that now is that time when we face that choice. We need to go toward spirit now. These prophecies were given to warn all people on the planet—not just the natives, but all the people on the planet. That way they can make the necessary

Photo 3. Sun Bear. *Photo courtesy of the Bear Tribe Medicine Society.*

changes in their lives. We have to shift our dependencies back to the Earth and back to each other as human beings. That's the only way we can go."

"For example, the prophecies of the Hopi people foresaw both world wars—to be fought against the sign of the four directions [Germany's swastika] and against the sun sign [Japan's rising sun]. They foresaw the invention of the automobile, the airplane, even the atom bomb. Ancient prophecies also spoke of a time when the sons of the white men would grow their hair long, wear beads, and live in communal societies. When that time came, according to the native prophets, the cleansing would be at hand. It happened in the sixties with flower power, the anti-Vietnam protesters, the Berkeley Free Speech Movement, and so on.

"Native prophecies say that mixed-blood and white people who grew their hair long and wore beads would come to native healers and ask for guidance—that they would be incarnations of the Indians slaughtered during the conquest of the continent. The prophecies say that they would return as rainbow people in bodies of different colors: red, white, yellow, and black. The old ones said that they would return and unite to help restore balance to the Earth.

"The story of these Rainbow Warriors is told by many peoples in many different ways. We feel that we are in that time now, when the Rainbow Warriors are coming about. The human race is no longer at a point where anybody can necessarily hold up their hand and say they are pure this or that. Even among the Indian tribes, you know, they might be all Indian, but they are Indian from two or three different tribal groups or something like that. So it's a time when we are having to acknowledge that we are all human beings upon the same planet, and that's what the Rainbow Warriors are all about.

"If you wake up and realize that we are Rainbow Warriors now, that we are a rainbow people upon the Earth, then the next step is becoming a spiritual warrior—someone who is willing to put their energy into something that helps to heal the Earth and restore the balance, and who is interested in doing that consistently, not just showing up for a weekend demonstration or something, but people who are willing to use their life energy to create a world of balance and harmony for our children after us."

It's the Way You Live Your Life

Oh Shinnah is a warrior woman. In her blood are mixed the traditions of the Tineh (Apache), the Mohawk, and the Scottish. She explains that her work in life, her challenge, is to be a warrior: speaking, singing, and acting on behalf of the Earth. To become recognized as a warrior, she had to go through all of the spiritual, physical, and mental training that Tineh men go through, including the Run for the Sun. That's an eight-to-ten-mile run attempted on the winter solstice. Candidates run the whole way before sunrise with water in their mouths. They must arrive at the Ceremony of the Moun-

Photo 4. Oh Shinnah. *Photo by Michael Silverwise.*

tain Spirits at the exact moment of sunrise to contribute their water. Oh Shinnah completed the run when she was eleven, and again at age forty just to prove she could still do it.

As with many indigenous teachers, Oh Shinnah is well aware of the rainbow prophecies. "The prophecies of many native peoples speak of the days of purification," she says. "We live them now. In these days we have the opportunity to do something real with our lives. It requires surrender and sacrifice to become a warrior; one must develop a strength so present that one will act, instead of react, always for the good of the whole, regardless of emotional impact. Our lives are short, but each life can make a difference."

Back in the 1970s, Oh Shinnah took part in the Longest Walk, a demonstration in which Indian people walked from California to Washington to protest the many injustices perpetrated against them by the government. At the end of the walk, some radical native people confronted her because she was not a full-blooded Native American.

Part of the concern of those who confronted Oh Shinnah was that she was sharing native ceremonies with nonnative people—something they felt should not happen. Oh Shinnah responded by saying that the wisdom and ceremonies she shares come from many traditions around the world and that she teaches very little of the native tradition, and then only what her mentors have given her authority to teach. "I must say I have mixed feelings about non-Indians leading Indian ceremonies. There is a prophecy that states a time would come when Indians would reincarnate on this planet as part of the dominant society, which is white society. The Indians' spirits would incarnate in the dominant society to change the attitude of that dominant society. So learning native ways is very natural to them.

"In this prophecy, these people would wear feathers and beads and communicate with the flowers. The flowers would guide them and support them as they walked their life paths. Once you learn to communicate with the flowers, you will be led from flower to flower to help you eliminate prejudice and hate from your life. This will also be a time when all the esoteric teachings of the world's traditions will be revealed, so there will be no secrets, no reason to fear each other or to be in conflict. This is clearly what is happening now.

"Not everyone has the strength or disposition to be a warrior. Many are Rainbow Walkers. They are the people who are walking simply and with dignity from this old time where there is hate and disrespect for the Earth. They are walking across the rainbow bridge to the new time, but they must leave the inconsistencies and the hate behind, or the seeds of hate will be planted in the new time where they will blossom later.

"People are being drawn to native ways because Mother Earth is experiencing trauma and calling to them. Native people are the keepers of Mother Earth. Our original instruction from Great Spirit was to take care of her. If a person has a sincere heart and wants to walk the path of the sacred, it should be accessible to them. The prophecies say we should do this. It is wrong for us not to share our spirituality with those who have lost theirs. But people should be very cautious with traditions they don't understand. People who participate in a ceremony and are not clear about what they are doing can create inharmonious results.

"As far as I'm concerned, it doesn't have anything to do with the color of your skin. It's the way you live your life. The only thing we have to give is the way we live our lives. If you live on this land, and you have ancestors sleeping in this land, I believe that makes you native to this land. It has nothing to do with the color of your skin. I was raised not to look at people racially. What I was taught is that we're flowers in the Great Spirit's garden. We share a common root, and the root is Mother Earth. The garden is beautiful because it has different colors in it, and those colors represent different traditions and cultural backgrounds."

A New People, A New World

Manitonquat, or Medicine Story, is the *powwah*, or spiritual leader, and the *minatou*, or keeper of the lore, for the Assonet band of the Wampanoag Nation. The ancestral land of his people is on the seacoast of Massachusetts. They are the Indians who met the Pilgrims, and who have, since antiquity, been known as the People of the Morning Light.

Medicine Story has traveled the world to tell his stories, which offer insights about how to live at peace with each other and the natural

Photo 5. Medicine Story (Manitonquat). *Photo by Linda Derman.*

world. One of his many adventures has been his involvement with a little-known social phenomenon that has happened every summer since the 1970s: the Rainbow Gatherings. Manitonquat has told the story of the gatherings many times.

"In 1972, I went to my first Rainbow Gathering and my life turned all around. Early in that year I received word of a great gathering that was planned to be held in the summer in the Colorado Rocky Mountains. Since it was to be people of all races, religions, nationalities, classes, and lifestyles, it was called a Gathering of the Rainbow Tribes. There was to be a walk, a pilgrimage to Table Mountain, a place sacred to the Arapaho. The people planned to fast and stay in silence all day on that mountain while praying for world peace and understanding.

"Now there are old prophecies that at the end of this world many people of many different nations and tribes would come together to seek a new world and a new way. This would be according to the vision the Creator placed in their hearts. Then, you know, seeing how sincerely they sought this, how deeply they desired it, the Great Spirit would hear the cries of their hearts and take pity on them. At that time, the prophecies said, the new world would be born in the midst of the old. This new world would be very small at first, like a newborn baby. But it would be full of life and learning and growth, full of trust and love, like a newborn. Because of this, the new world wouldn't hate the dying old world, but instead learn how to survive and become strong within it. It was said that the sign the Creator would send of this new beginning would be a white buffalo.

"More than twenty thousand people came to that first gathering, and everyone was treated with respect. It was wonderful. One night it rained. The next day, when we came out in the meadow, we saw that a huge patch of white snow on the side of the mountain that faced us had been eaten away and carved into the perfect shape of a white buffalo. People began to cheer and sing, and many of them wept joyfully.

"Then, starting at midnight on the third of July, everybody began a walk over the eight miles to Table Mountain. All night long that line moved in silence, carrying candles and torches. At dawn, thousands of people stood still upon the mountain, people who had come from all over the world to be together and share that moment, to watch the sun rise on a new day, a new people, a new world.

"People stayed together all day on that mountain. We fasted and stayed in silence until, sometime after noon, someone started singing an Arapaho chant. All of us took up that chant to honor the traditional caretakers of that land. When we left that gathering, everyone had the feeling that something very important had happened, and was happening all over the world. No one could say exactly what it was, or knew what to do about it. So everyone went home and went on with their business. But the next summer a lot of the people decided the only way they could learn what to do with this new energy was to gather again and keep on gathering until the spirit directed something different. That's how it's been. Ever since, the Rainbow World Family Gathering of the Tribes has been held during the first week of July."

The dream of the Rainbow Gathering sprang from the cultural watershed of Woodstock, when a commune named the Hog Farm and a clown named Wavy Gravy helped feed four hundred thousand people. That spiritual service was immensely inspiring to the founders of the Rainbow Gathering.

The founders saw the rainbow as a sign of unity for all people in the universal family. As the fliers for the annual gathering proclaim, "The people who gather are a tribe not of blood but of spirit, for all are born into it. We are bound together by our desire to live in peace, to be in the cathedral of nature, and to heal ourselves through union with the earthly mother and the heavenly father. The Rainbow Gathering is an opportunity to celebrate human diversity, to venerate the Earth, to deepen connections, and to party—to share a community that is beyond the rules of violence, prejudice, and caste." Each summer the gathering moves to a new state and sets up camp in one of the national forests. At the gatherings there is no exchange of money. The Rainbow Tribe relies on cooperation, respect, goodwill, and equal rights. And for at least one week every summer, it works.

Medicine Story attended the first fifteen Rainbow Gatherings consecutively and is one of its grandfathers. He has also attended Rainbow Gatherings in Europe and at the Arctic Circle. As he has matured, the gatherings and the vision they represent have been deeply important to him.

"One reason my life turned around," he explains, "was this vision of twenty thousand people getting together on top of a mountain praying in silence for a new world to be ushered in. The whole thing was so powerful. I knew something was happening. I didn't know what, or how, but I knew I had to be a part of it. Also, I met a number of young Indians who, although they weren't very traditional, came from people who were traditional and had their traditions together. They invited me to their reservation, to the Sun Dance and the sweatlodge and things like that. And so I opened up into a whole world of traditional old ways that I knew nothing about. So those two things came together at the same time, this rainbow communal world vision, and the old ways, finding that there were still the old ways, and going to seek them out. I kept balancing those two things."

The Rainbow Seeds

Photo 6. Hunbatz Men. *Author photo.*

The indigenous people of the Americas say they have known for many hundreds of years that there were people in all Four Directions and that Indian people long ago visited other places to study and exchange art, science, and other ideas. The native culture of the Americas, though, began to change drastically with the coming of Columbus, who proved to be the first of many pitiless men, senselessly murdering thousands of peaceful Indians on his voyages of discovery and exploitation.

In the South, the genocide of indigenous people in Mexico began in earnest when Hernando Cortés arrived in Veracruz, Mexico, on Good Friday, A.D. 1519, with a Roman Catholic priest at his side. The indigenous people say they knew that someone like Cortés would come, and thanks to their elaborate calendars they knew to the day when this would happen. They had, in fact, sent scouts to Veracruz to greet Cortés, for they hoped he would be the return of the great spiritual messenger Quetzalcoatl, whose symbol is the Rainbow Feathered Serpent. Instead, Cortés proved to be the bringer of sorrows.

The Aztec emperor Montezuma II felt his power was threatened. He was frightened by the omens and did everything short of violence to prevent Cortés from advancing inland. But Cortés did advance, and the rest of the story is one of bloodshed, disease, and trouble as the native people were systematically killed or enslaved. According to Hunbatz Men, a shaman and daykeeper for the Mayan people of Mexico's Yucatán peninsula, "the problem is that when the Europeans came to visit they did not respect anything that was already here. The native people could have built more weapons when they became aware that the white men were coming, but the elders knew this was not the path of wisdom. They took another approach."

According to the elaborate and sophisticated Mayan calendars that Hunbatz has studied his whole life, just as Cortés was stepping ashore, a long cycle of thirteen heavens was coming to an end. For the Maya, it was the beginning of a dark cycle of pain, suffering, sadness, and death—the beginning of the reign of Xibalba, the world of the Nine Lords of Darkness, the Nine Bolontikus, the Nine Hells. Though in many respects the time of the Nine Hells has been a time of great darkness, the Maya have also seen it as a time to cross-fertilize the seeds of the Four Directions and races of the planet. This difficult task they have seen as the beginning of a new nation of multicolored beings. The seeds of the Four Directions have mixed together to create the first rainbow people.

Before the arrival of the Spanish, the Maya and many other Native American groups entrusted certain families with sacred information and the responsibility to keep it secret so that it could not be destroyed or abused. Guidance to take this action came from a council of elders that had been meeting for thousands of years before the Europeans came to Turtle Island. The council was made up of representatives from all of the Indian nations from Nicaragua north to the Arctic Circle. From dreams, visions, and prophecies, the elders of the council had become aware that the newcomers would try to change their religion, so they kept the most profound parts of their religion and science in their hearts and did not speak about them to anyone.

More than five hundred years ago, Hunbatz Men's family was entrusted with safekeeping part of this wisdom tradition. He is the contemporary holder of the lineage, although now, because it is time, he has begun to share the secrets. "The eyes of modern civilization see only a short span of time," he says. "To the European-American culture, five hundred years seems to be a lot of time. But five hundred years is nothing in the eyes of the Maya.

"It is written in time and in the memory of the Indian peoples that our sun will rise again, that we will be able to reestablish our culture: its arts, sciences, mathematics, and religion. Mayan knowledge will come forward again. It is for this reason that we of the Amerindian communities are once again uniting to reestablish our entire culture."

THREE

Rainbow Heritage,
Rainbow Destiny

*N*ative American elders are not the only visionaries who have walked and worked on this continent. As has been documented extensively, the founders of the United States were also people of high vision and acute spiritual awareness. They had respect for both tradition and the future. While the Constitution, the Bill of Rights, and the Declaration of Independence are evidence of their vision and wisdom, some of the spiritual foundation they created for the United States has remained hidden. It just isn't taught in high school civics courses.

The founders of the United States were steeped in the ancient spiritual traditions of the European continent. Of the fifty-six signers of the Declaration of Independence, fifty-one belonged to the brotherhood of Freemasons, which was established in America under the guidance of Francis Bacon. Bacon saw the colonies as a testing ground for the spiritual principles of government that had been passed down from the ancient mystery schools in Greece, Egypt, and Chaldea. Many of the founders were well versed in numerology, astrology, and other spiritual sciences—disciplines that have since seemingly vanished from the Masonic tradition and been condemned by the hierarchy of technology.

Many of the metaphysical dimensions of the nation's founding are insightfully chronicled by Corrine McLaughlin and Gordon Davidson in their book *The Spiritual Heritage and Destiny of America*. They mention, for example, that when the cornerstone of the Capitol

Figure 2. George Washington Inaugurates U.S. Capitol. *Wearing a Masonic apron, George Washington lays the cornerstone for the U.S. Capitol building. Fresco in the U.S. Capitol by Alan Cox, reprinted courtesy of the Architect of the Capitol.*

building was laid, the ceremony closely followed a Masonic ritual. George Washington himself presided over the event wearing a powdered wig and Masonic apron.

Development of the U.S. Constitution was a conscious spiritual undertaking. The founders of the United States sought to join the European traditions in subtle but meaningful ways with the traditions of Turtle Island. While the European heritage offered order, intellectual rigor, and justice, the Turtle Island tradition offered democracy and tolerance for differences in race, religion, and point of view—virtues lacking in the European dispensation of the 1700s.

The essential message of the rainbow is both implicit and explicit in the nation's spiritual history and destiny. The Legend of the Rainbow Warriors suggests that the true destiny of the nation is to synthesize for posterity the cultural heritage of the various races: the intellect and will of the light-skinned people, the intuition and spiritual awareness so highly developed in the red-skinned people, and the gifts of the yellow- and black-skinned people as well. This synthesis, naturally, must be based on tolerance and mutual respect.

Because the founders recognized the essential importance of tolerance, they began the Declaration of Independence with the statement: "We hold these truths to be self-evident: that all men are created equal . . ." Ultimately, so esteemed was tolerance that the founders put a guarantee of it in the Bill of Rights, and the nation fought a bloody Civil War over it. Later, as we moved into the twentieth century, we adopted the "melting pot" image as a popular mythology. What has emerged from the melting pot, however, is hardly homogenous; rather, it is a polyglot of differences, often in conflict, but with the potential to complement each other—a nascent rainbow culture.

An Angelic Presence

While he was encamped at Valley Forge with the Revolutionary Army in the winter of 1777, George Washington, first president of the United States, had a powerful, prophetic vision of an angelic presence. He reported in a letter to a friend that one cold night while he was alone, an archangel appeared and showed him a vision of three great crises of the republic: the American Revolution, the Civil War, and a third crisis, even greater than the previous two.

This story is documented in the December 1880 edition of the *National Tribune*. Based on the word of Anthony Sherman, who was at Valley Forge with Washington, the paper reported that an angelic presence appeared before Washington in the winter of 1777 while he was working alone at his desk. Although some historians have expressed doubts about the authenticity of this experience, according to Sherman, Washington himself made a careful record of the encounter:

> I do not know whether it is owing to the anxiety of my mind or what, but this afternoon, as I was sitting at this table engaged in preparing a dispatch, something seemed to disturb me. Looking up, I beheld standing opposite me a singularly beautiful

female. . . . I would have risen but the riveted gaze of the being before me rendered volition impossible. I assayed once more to address her, but my tongue had become useless. Even thought in itself had become paralyzed. A new influence, mysterious, potent, irresistible, took possession of me. All I could do was to gaze steadily, vacantly, at my unknown visitant. Gradually the surrounding atmosphere seemed as though becoming filled with sensations, and grew luminous. Everything about me seemed to rarify, the mysterious visitor herself becoming more airy and yet more distinct to my sight than before. . . .

Presently I heard a voice saying, "Son of the republic, look and learn," while at the same time my visitor extended her arm eastwardly. . . .

The scene instantly began to fade and dissolve, and I at last saw nothing but the rising, curling vapor I at first beheld. This also disappearing, I found myself once more gaping upon the mysterious visitor, who, in the same voice I had heard before, said, "Son of the republic, what you have seen is thus interpreted. Three great perils will come upon the republic. . . . The most fearful is the third. The help against the third peril comes in the shape of Divine Assistance, passing which the whole world united shall not prevail against her. Let every child of the republic learn to live for his God, his land, and union." With these words the vision vanished, and I started from my seat and felt that I had seen a vision wherein had been shown to me the birth, progress and destiny of the United States.

The third great peril shown to Washington by the angelic presence is by far the most enigmatic. According to Sherman, Washington's notes give no indications to suggest what it might be or when it might occur.

Shared Traditions

George Washington, Thomas Jefferson, Benjamin Franklin, and the other founders were deeply inspired in their work not only by the European esoteric tradition but also by the Confederacy of the Haudenosaunee, known more popularly as the League of Iroquois Indians or the Iroquois Confederacy, which inhabits the territory now known as New York state and southern Canada.

According to the oral history of the Haudenosaunee, long before the light-skinned race arrived on Turtle Island, the indigenous peoples of the Northeast had reached a crisis. Blood feuds between clans and a harsh, vindictive justice had made the society unsafe. At this time, about three hundred years before the arrival of the Europeans, a male child was born to a woman of the Wyandot people living on the north shore of Lake Ontario. The child grew up to be a wise leader, so revered that his name is now spoken only in ceremony. He is generally referred to simply as the Peacemaker.

With his companion Hiawatha, the Peacemaker was able to "straighten the minds" of the most angry and fearsome of the people. He brought all the people together under a set of principles known now as the Great Law. The Great Law embodies many noble ideas, including the following:

> The Giver of Life—the Creator—did not intend that people abuse one another. Therefore, human societies must form governments that prevent the abuse of human beings by other human beings and that ensure peace among nations and peoples.
>
> Peace is the product of a society that strives to establish reason and righteousness. "Righteousness" refers to the shared ideology of the people using their purest and most unselfish minds.
>
> All people have a right to the things they need to survive—even those who do not or cannot work. No people or person has a right to deprive others of these things: food, clothing, shelter, and protection.
>
> Human beings should use every effort to sit in council about, arbitrate, and negotiate their differences. Force should be resorted to only as a defense against the certain use of force.
>
> Chiefs or leaders are the servants of the people. Everyone has a right and a responsibility to participate in the workings of the government.

The Peacemaker's concepts of moral justice were way ahead of his time. He also created a system of governmental organization that was a complex formulation of participatory, rather than representative, government. When the idea of the United Nations was proposed at the end of World War II, researchers were asked to find models in history for such an organization. The only working model they could find was the Iroquois Confederacy.

Likewise, earlier in history, when the founders of the United States set out to create a new form of democratic government, a form that the Eurpeans had not yet experienced, they looked to the wisdom of the Peacemaker and the example of the Iroquois Confederacy. Many of the spiritual and legal principles that guided the Confederacy then—and still guide it to this day—were borrowed for the Constitution of the United States.

Historian Gregory Schaff, Ph.D., author of *Wampum Belts and Peace Trees: George Morgan, Native Americans and Revolutionary Diplomacy*, conducted fourteen years of research on the authenticity of this piece of history. Schaff's work culminated in his 1990 testimony before the U.S. Senate Committee on Indian Affairs. As a result of his convincing evidence and testimony, Congress passed a resolution that was signed by President George Bush. In the resolution, for the first time in history, the U.S. government officially recognized that the main ideas for the U.S. Constitution actually came from the American Indian people and that the very structure of U.S. government was explicitly modeled after the Iroquois Confederacy.

The Great Seal

If symbols are the language of dreams, and if the founders of the United States were motivated by an American dream, then the Great Seal that appears on the back of every dollar bill can be considered a definitive symbolic expression of that dream. This national emblem can help us understand the spiritual traditions our founders built upon, the future they envisioned, and our place in that future.

In 1782, Benjamin Franklin, Thomas Jefferson, and Charles Thompson were commissioned by the first Congress to design the official emblem of the new nation. Their commission became the Great Seal of the United States, the official impression that attests to the authenticity and legality of any agreement entered into by the

United States government. The seal has been in continuous, legal use since it was established.

The Great Seal is a circle with striking images on both its front and back. For the front of the seal, Franklin, Jefferson, and Thompson selected the eagle. Long sacred to Native Americans, the eagle represents power and spiritual vision. It flies higher than all other birds and is the only creature that can look directly into the sun. The eagle on the seal grasps a banner in its mouth reading *E Pluribus Unum*, meaning "out of many, one."

The reverse of the seal bears the image of a four-sided pyramid, representing the material world. The all-seeing Eye of God at the capstone of the pyramid suggests the founders' intention that spiritual vision guide the affairs of the nation at all times. The location of the eye further suggests that spiritual vision be a guide for and be given priority over the abundant material life symbolized by the pyramid. This reverse side of the Great Seal makes it plain that the founders saw the creation of the United States as a revolutionary undertaking. The motto they placed beneath the pyramid reads *Novus Ordo Seclorum*, "the new order of the ages."

In esoteric studies, thirteen is a number that signifies transformation. Thirteen is used thirteen times on the Great Seal of the United

Figure 3. The Great Seal of the United States. *The official emblem of the nation, designed by Benjamin Franklin, Thomas Jefferson, and Charles Thompson. Tradition holds that the seal offers a unified set of symbolic clues to the spiritual intention of the founders.*

States: in the number of stars, arrows, olive leaves, berries, levels of the pyramid, letters in *E Pluribus Unum*, letters in *Annuit Coeptis* ("the Eye of Providence favors our undertaking") and so forth. Was it a coincidence that the United States started with thirteen colonies?

Although it was designed more than two hundred years ago, the Great Seal was seldom seen until Henry Wallace, the secretary of agriculture under President Franklin D. Roosevelt, suggested during the 1930s that it be placed on the dollar bill. Wallace was a student of the ageless wisdom and appreciated the importance of the Great Seal's symbolism.

Corinne McLaughlin and Gordon Davidson are founding members of the Sirius Community in Shutesbury, Massachusetts, and have taught at American University and Hampshire College. They are scholars who have investigated the nation's early days extensively, pondered its mysteries, and expounded upon them in their book *The Spiritual Heritage and Destiny of America*. As they see it, our national spiritual destiny is "to demonstrate to the world the unity of many races and many religions and classes of people living together in cooperation and harmony, respecting the divine presence in all life. . . . Our destiny is also to bring forth the divine aspect within matter."

McLaughlin and Davidson write that "we as Americans have gone deeply into materialism and are now learning the lessons of working creatively and lovingly with matter. America must transform materialism into unselfishness and commitment to the good of the whole." They believe that the separation of church and state in our founding documents was not meant to remove Spirit from government but rather to free the state from the control of dogmatic religion and to allow a more universal expression of Spirit.

Points on the Eagle's Compass

As we approach the millennium, there are few elected leaders in the United States articulating the high vision that animated the founders of the nation. Perhaps this is not so surprising. According to the mythology of the rainbow, we are in a time of transition, just now entering a New Age, a new order of the ages. The rainbow legend avers that this age is not about great leaders but is rather a time

Figure 4. Messenger. *The American Bald Eagle is a symbol of central importance for both ancient and modern America. Flying higher than any of the other winged ones, the eagle is the only creature of flesh and blood that can look directly into the sun. For ancient America, the eagle represents a spiritual messenger who is said to bring the sacred pipe, a symbol joining of the basic forces of the universe: the bowl of the pipe represents the feminine forces; the stem represents the masculine forces. Four colored streamers on the stem honor the four races of humanity living in harmony. In modern America, all over the continent, the eagle retains high respect as a symbol for life, liberty, and the pursuit of happiness. Painting by Scott Guynup.*

when individuals and groups will be called upon to to exercise intelligence, intuition, and free will in the service of humanity. Each must find his or her own way to serve family, neighborhood, nation, and planet. In the context of this legend, the U.S. national challenge contains two seemingly paradoxical elements for individual citizens: the urge to be free, unique individuals and at the same time the impulse to find a path of service that benefits all the people.

While the United States may have powerful symbols like the soaring eagle and the Great Seal, the mythology of the rainbow suggests that we are not likely to have many national leaders who are capable of focusing our attention on the inner meaning of those symbols and the absolute importance of embodying the qualities they symbolize. According to the Legend of the Rainbow Warriors, there is little point in waiting for a George Washington, an Abraham Lincoln, or even a Florence Nightingale to come to our rescue. They are unlikely to arrive. We are all going to have to find our own ways through this transition to a new time, using the spiritual resources that lie within each of us.

What happens within the Earth or within a melting pot is frequently turbulent. When heat is applied directly, alchemical processes take place. Strong currents begin to mingle. There can be violent collisions, explosions, and rapid shifts. In our era—not only in the United States but also throughout the world—the melting pot is at a rolling boil. Racial, religious, economic, and environmental elements are all mingling furiously in the pot.

As we pass through this crucible of history, if enough Americans accept and consciously seek to fulfill the founders' dream of alchemy and union, to reestablish the nation on a path toward its destiny, then in all likelihood the United States will again find its place in history. As in the past, the nation will become a beacon, an inspiration to other peoples and other nations.

The beacon is an image much in keeping with two of the most popular national symbols: Liberty, who lifts her light by the eastern gate, and the eagle, who soars overhead. For thousands of years, soaring eagles showed the way onward and upward for the people of Turtle Island. Eagles still fly today, albeit over a ravaged Earth.

FOUR

A Legend Aroused

*I*n the early 1970s, under circumstances both curious and compelling, the Legend of the Rainbow Warriors came to life. Through an environmental organization that came to be known as Greenpeace, the legend found its heartbeat first in Canada, then in the United States, and finally throughout the world.

The saga began in late 1969 when the U.S. government detonated a one-megaton nuclear bomb on a tiny island named Amchitka, off the west coast of Alaska. As it happens, this was—and still is—one of the most earthquake-sensitive areas in the world. For many observers, it made little sense to explode massive nuclear bombs along the delicate fault line extending from Amchitka to the Alaskan mainland. The nuclear blast in 1969 did not cause an earthquake, but it did raise a groundswell of protest in Canada and the United States.

Then, in 1971, the United States announced plans for another test blast on Amchitka—code named Cannikin—that was to be five times stronger than the previous one. Many people believed something had to be done to stop it. Among those who felt called to action were Canadians Jim and Marie Bohlen, Irving and Dorothy Stowe, and Paul Cote. They formed the Don't Make a Wave Committee, whose name was intended to remind people that if the nuclear blast caused an earthquake, it would probably also bring a *tsunami*—a seismic tidal wave of tremendous power.

Members of the committee began attending public hearings to protest the proposed five-megaton Cannikin blast and then decided to take direct action. Specifically, they elected to secure a boat and sail directly to Amchitka to blockade the blast.

At one of the planning meetings held in Vancouver, British Columbia, the group searched for another name for the organization. As Jim Bohlen later explained, "The Don't Make a Wave Committee was a lot of words that didn't mean much. People didn't really relate to it, didn't know what it meant. So the group was trying to think of something that was more generic, that people could understand." Eventually, a young Canadian social worker named Bill Darnell came up with the name "Greenpeace." Because the name conveyed the group's broad goals succinctly, it stuck.

At 4 p.m. on September 15, 1971, after months of preparation and extensive media coverage, the ship *Phyllis Cormack*—now sporting the logo of Greenpeace—hoisted a green triangular sail and slipped away from the dock in Vancouver. The first of hundreds of Greenpeace adventures had begun.

Just Before It Was Too Late

Among the small band of activists on board the *Phyllis Cormack* was Robert Hunter, a columnist for the *Vancouver Sun*. Since the first nuclear blast at Amchitka, he had written many an impassioned article about the environment and the state of the world.

On October 2, 1969, he had written a column almost prophetic in its grasp of what lay ahead: "Politicians, take note. There is a power out there in suburbia, so far harnessed only to charity drives, campaigns and PTAs, which, if ever properly brought to bear on the great problems of the day, will have an impact so great the result of its being detonated (like the Amchitka A-Bomb test) cannot be predicted."

Back in 1969, Hunter had a farm in western Canada. One day a vagabond dulcimer maker came through and presented him with a slim volume entitled *Warriors of the Rainbow,* by William Willoya and Vinson Brown. The itinerant craftsman told him the little book would change his life, and then he left, never to be seen again.

Hunter took the book with him when he boarded that first Greenpeace expedition. The book contained an ancient prophecy that seemed particularly relevant to the ship's crew. The book told the story of how a Cree grandmother named Eyes of Fire had predicted that there would come a time when the Earth would be ravaged of its resources, the sea blackened, the streams poisoned, and the deer made to drop dead in their tracks—all due to greed and technology. Eyes of Fire had seen that at the time of these happenings, the Indian people would have all but completely lost their spirit. But, just before it was too late, they would find their spirit again and would begin to teach others how to have reverence for Mother Earth. Under the symbol of the rainbow, all the races of the world would band together to spread these great teachings. The teachers would be the Warriors of the Rainbow, and they would ultimately, after a great struggle, bring an end to the desecration of the Earth.

Robert Hunter was struck by the connections between this Indian legend, the reality of the world condition, and the work that he found himself and Greenpeace doing. He passed his copy of the book around the ship so others could read it. The next day, rainbows appeared several times as the boat chugged through a maze of inlets and channels. Hunter later wrote, "It all did seem somehow magical." There they were, journeying over the ocean waters on a campaign, just as the legend prophesied, to help save Mother Earth.

Did Hunter and the crew members believe the Cree legend—that one day the Indians would find their lost spirit and teach the light-skinned people how to have reverence for Mother Earth, and that people would go forth as Warriors of the Rainbow to protect the natural world? According to *The Greenpeace Story*, by Michael Brown and John May, on some days Hunter believed the legend and on other days he did not. In the beginning, he found being part of Greenpeace difficult and discouraging. There were many obstacles and tremendous resistance to what the members were trying to do. In the early 1970s, environmentalists were widely considered to be the lunatic fringe.

"The Cree legend says nothing about how difficult the passage to the new time will be," Hunter has explained. "It does not tell what the voyage from a world bent on destroying itself to a world committed to saving itself will be like. It just says it will happen."

In later years, Robert Hunter became Greenpeace's liaison with the Native American community. From time to time, during the years 1973 through 1977, he served as chairman for Greenpeace.

That first voyage of the *Phyllis Cormack*, by all accounts, was tremendously challenging. The ship itself was plagued by mechanical failures, the crew became weary, and they were arrested by the U.S. Coast Guard for failing to notify customs of their arrival in U.S. waters. The weather turned bad, and, frustratingly, the U.S. government postponed the atomic blast several times. Many crew members had to get back to their jobs. Morale waned. And so, on October 12, 1972, they voted to return to Vancouver.

However, on the way back, the crew was invited to dock at Kodiak Island, where a banquet sponsored by the city honored their bravery. Later, in a stunning moment of mythic coincidence, at Alert Bay they were greeted by the Kwakiutl Indians, who annointed them at a sacred ceremony in their longhouse and made them honorary tribal members.

Oddly, though the isolated crew had become discouraged and had developed a sense of defeat, their voyage had been front-page

Photo 7. Greenpeace Initiation into the Kwakiutl Tribe. *At the end of the first Greenpeace expedition in 1971, the members of the crew were invited to the longhouse of the Kwakiutl people to be initiated as honorary members of the tribe. Photo by Robert Keziere/Greenpeace.*

news in Canada. They had generated tremendous goodwill, not only in the North, but also in the United States and elsewhere around the world. In fact, public support had been so strong that, back in British Columbia, Irving Stowe had been able to raise the money for another, faster Greenpeace ship. Just as the *Phyllis Cormack* returned home, the *Edgewater Fortune* set off with another crew for a second try at blocking the explosion at Amchitka. However, on November 6, 1971, while the *Edgewater Fortune* was still seven hundred miles away, the five-megaton nuclear bomb was detonated.

While the fledgling Greenpeace organization had been unable to stop the blast, it did succeed in its larger goal. The protests had grown so strong that the U.S. government decided to stop its nuclear tests at Amchitka.

The Rainbow Goes to Sea

At the beginning of 1978, a growing Greenpeace, by now an international organization, purchased a twenty-year-old Scottish trawler named the *Sir William Hardy*. The 160-foot ship was moved to a new dock, refitted for environmental work, and painted white and dark green. A bright rainbow was emblazoned on her side, and a dove carrying an olive branch was painted across her bow. She was then rechristened the *Rainbow Warrior*.

On May 15, 1978, Greenpeace's new ship sailed out under the Tower Bridge of London on her maiden voyage. Shortly thereafter, in the first of many exploits, she intercepted the *Gem*, a British-owned nuclear-waste ship. The *Gem* was on its way to foul the international waters of the ocean with two thousand tons of radioactive waste—waste that would remain radioactive for millennia. That same year, the *Rainbow Warrior* successfully opposed the Norwegian hunt of grey seals on the Orkney Islands and set off on campaigns to help save the harp seals, the whales, and the dolphins. It also initiated efforts against oil, chemical, and nuclear pollution.

Greenpeace has become famous—and in some corporate headquarters infamous—for its daring exploits and dramatic stunts, all intended to call attention to the systematic industrial destruction of the Earth and the creatures who share life upon it—the poisoning of the world with toxic substances and practices. In accordance with the group's central philosophy, all of the confrontations have been nonviolent. Following is a small sample of the thousands of actions Greenpeace has undertaken all over the world:

- They parachuted into the construction site of the largest nuclear power plant in the world, the Darlington Generating Station in Ontario, Canada.

- They marched to and then occupied the Trident nuclear submarine base in Washington state.

- They released three hundred dolphins trapped in nets off the Japanese coast before fishermen returned to massacre them.

- They climbed the scaffolding surrounding the Statue of Liberty in New York Harbor while the statue was being restored and hung a huge banner from it proclaiming, "Give Me Liberty from Nuclear Weapons. Stop Testing."

- They plugged the waste discharge pipes of the Monsanto chemical plant in Boston, Massachusetts, to prevent the daily fouling of Boston Harbor.

- They scaled industrial smokestacks across Europe to hang banners that spelled out "STOP"—a demand for an end to the steady onslaught of bitter emissions that causes the rains to turn dark and acid.

Early in the 1990s, Greenpeace began calling for a fifth Geneva Convention to put the environment under international legal protection in times of armed conflict. The previous four Geneva conventions have provided international legal safeguards to protect minimum human values in times of war.

As of 1992, Greenpeace has five million supporters in thirty countries and forty-six offices in twenty-six countries, with about a thousand full-time staff members connected by an international computer network. The organization is actively involved in some thirty international conventions for the protection of the environment.

Over the years, Greenpeace has consistently worked in the face of danger. While boldly confrontational, the group has remained nonviolent. It has sought to radically transform our understanding of the world and the direction in which it is heading. As the group's official history states, their message is simple and powerful, an echo of the Great Law of the Iroquois people: "Everyone has the right to clean water, fresh air, and a safe future."

Rainbow's End?

In July of 1985, the *Rainbow Warrior* arrived at Auckland Harbor in New Zealand on its campaign for a nuclear-free Pacific. The ship's crew was planning to gather support from well-wishers in New Zealand and then to join a peace fleet that would sail to the Moruroa Atoll, where France had been exploding nuclear bombs steadily since 1966. Greenpeace was making this protest for the fifth time in thirteen years, and apparently the French had run out of patience with the organization's interference.

The ship received a rousing welcome when it arrived at the harbor. But then, four days later, at about 11:45 pm on July 10, 1985, an

Photo 8. The *Rainbow Warrior*. *Agents of the French government planted bombs on board the* Rainbow Warrior *on July 10, 1986. The explosion sank the ship and killed Greenpeace photographer Fernando Pereira. Photo © 1985 Miller/Greenpeace.*

explosion ripped a six-by-eight foot hole in the hull of the *Rainbow Warrior* while it lay at anchor at Marsden Wharf in Auckland Harbor.

After the explosion, Greenpeace photographer Fernando Pereira ran to the door of the engine room to survey the scene. He turned swiftly and started back to his cabin, apparently to rescue his cameras. It was a fatal turn. Moments later, a second explosion rocked the *Rainbow Warrior*, and the boat sank, incredibly fast. Thirteen people on board scrambled ashore quickly and safely, but hours later, divers from the New Zealand Navy found Pereira's body. The cause of his death was listed as drowning.

Despite the organization's astounding record of dramatic, risky, and confrontational tactics, Pereira became the first member of Greenpeace ever to be killed while working on a campaign. At the time of the bombing, New Zealand's prime minister, David Lange, quickly labeled the incident "a major criminal act with terrorist overtones." Terrorism indeed—perhaps the first major act of terrorism against the defenders of the Earth. In response to the sinking, Greenpeace International chairman David McTaggart offered two blunt sentences: "We campaign against violence. We will not be stopped by it."

Two days after the sinking, a couple, both officers in the French military, was arrested and charged with murder and arson in connection with the bombing. As the investigation proceeded, it was revealed that the plot to sink the *Rainbow Warrior* extended to the highest levels of French government. The scandal implicated not only French agents Dominique Prieur and Alain Mafart, but also Admiral Pierre Lacoste, head of the French secret service, and the French minister of defense, Charles Hernu. President François Mitterand himself was nearly forced to resign.

You Can't Sink a Rainbow

Eventually, the *Rainbow Warrior* was towed out to sea and sunk eighty feet beneath the waters of New Zealand's Matauri Bay. The boat forms an artificial reef there, a sanctuary for marine life.

Four years to the day after the bombing, on July 10, 1989, Greenpeace launched a new ship, also named the *Rainbow Warrior*, in

Hamburg Harbor, West Germany. At the launching ceremonies, Rebecca Johnson, head of Greenpeace's campaign against nuclear testing, said, "The name *Rainbow Warrior* symbolizes that you cannot sink an idea, or remove it by force."

The new boat is a 181-foot Scottish trawler built in 1957. It cost $4 million to purchase and refit the ship. To reduce energy demand, Greenpeace had the boat redesigned to carry three masts and specially designed sails. The arrangement yields fuel savings of as much as 80 percent. Greenpeace paid for the new flagship with some of the $8.2 million in damages it received from the French government.

Like its predecessor, the new *Rainbow Warrior* is based in the Pacific, where it sails to combat nuclear and chemical pollution and to thwart drift-net fishing by Japan, Korea, and Taiwan.

When the first *Rainbow Warrior* sank in Auckland Harbor, it took with it any illusions that the global healing process would be an easy task. As the smoke cleared from the explosions, it became starkly ap-

Photo 9. The new *Rainbow Warrior. The new Greenpeace ship sails the seas to call attention to the nuclear and chemical dumping that have fouled waters around the world. Photo by Culley/Greenpeace © 1989.*

parent that the struggle would be, in essence, a war for the fate of the Earth. Could that war be fought and won with peaceful means—with confrontational but nonviolent means? Could the rainbow really come to life?

Mythology may have been a helpful source of inspiration for Greenpeace in the beginning, but the organization was founded in response to real world problems, and it has remained clearly focused on those problems. Greenpeace has, appropriately, maintained a low-key emphasis on the legend, directing its collective resources to halting the poisons that glut our world while promoting technologies that are in harmony with the Earth—technologies that will make a clean life possible for future generations.

⟨⟨⟨ FIVE ⟩⟩⟩

A Calendar Calls

*T*hrough the courageous actions of Greenpeace, thousands of people were awakened to the perilous condition of the Earth's environment and spurred to direct, creative action. However, toxins continued to glut the earth, the air, and the water, and millions of people slumbered through the 1970s and 1980s as if the problems of the Earth belonged only to others. Then, midway through 1987, something happened that woke up many more people—something that acted, in a sense, as a cosmic alarm clock for millions of Rainbow Warriors.

Though the terms *New Age* and *Age of Aquarius* are well known, if not particularly well understood, few people have ever heard of the term *Age of Flowers.*Yet, if there is substance to one of the central legends of the land now known as America, the Age of Flowers began in the summer of 1987 with an event that many Native American wisdom keepers say was of critical importance.

According to students of Turtle Island's legends and prophecies, the Age of Flowers began in August of 1987 with a sharp acceleration of the energy at work in the world. This acceleration initiated a period of intense change that, it has been said, will shake the world for twenty-five years, until A.D. 2012, as the old gives way to the new.

Arising from the ancient cultures of Central America, the prophecies concerning the transition from one age to another are recorded in what have come to be known as the Mayan and Aztec calendars—works of high mathematical sophistication. Because of their scientific elegance and the depth of the information they contain, these

47

calendars, as well as the pyramids of the Americas, are considered by metaphysical scholars to be the principal repositories of the esoteric teachings of the Western Hemisphere. The southlands of Turtle Island, home to some twenty thousand magnificent pyramids and temples, can be seen as the Egypt of the Americas. To be understood, the native prophecies from these southlands require a historical context, one provided by a part of the American heritage given scant attention in textbooks.

Figure 5. Keeper of Sacred Time. *The great circular Aztec calendar has been recognized by mathematicians as being more precise, accurate, and sophisticated than the Gregorian calendar used by modern Western culture. Along with the seventeen calendars of the Maya, who are the sacred keepers of time, the Aztec calendar pointed to a major change beginning in 1987. Reprinted from* American Indian Design & Decoration *by LeRoy H. Appleton courtesy of Dover Publications, Inc.*

The Lord of the Dawn

More than a thousand years ago in the land now known as Mexico, the Toltec tribe was led by a great king and prophet named Quetzalcoatl. His symbol was a serpent covered with green feathers, representing the union of Earth and Spirit. Around his head, like an aura, was a half-circle crown of rainbow-hued feathers, sparkling with the full spectrum of color. Called the Lord of the Dawn, Quetzalcoatl was thought to be a Divine Son who was carrying out the will of the Creator.

This king was described as a white man, with a beard, who wore long robes and taught of one supreme God. He also gave the Toltecs many material gifts, such as their calendar, and instructed them in all manner of arts, sciences, and social customs. Members of the Mormon Church, and many other people, believe that Quetzalcoatal was actually Christ visiting the Americas during what are known as his lost years, from the ages of twelve through thirty. In the *Book of Mormon* and other publications, the Mormons assert this claim in some detail. As with Jesus Christ, a central part of the myth of Quetzalcoatl is his promise, at death, to return from the East when the world is great need.

Further south in Central America, Quetzalcoatl is known as Kukulcan or Gucumatz. South America was also visited by a teacher of similar description who goes by a variety of names: Sume in Brazil, Bochia in Columbia, and Con-tici or Viracocha in Peru. In North America, this teacher is often referred to simply as the Pale One.

Though the myths of the Americas are in some ways indistinct, many students of these continents would agree that Quetzalcoatl represents the Americas' most spectacular culture hero. His legend is certainly the one with the most widespread influence. In the regions we know today as Mexico, he taught a religion of love and formed two holy orders: the Jaguar Knights and the Eagle Knights. Like the famed Knights of the Round Table—and at about the same period in history—these Central American knights were dedicated to the search for spiritual strength and to performing deeds of honor, mercy, and kindness. Along with all who believed in Quetzalcoatl's teachings, they became members of the Fellowship of the Tree of Life, symbolized by a real tree in Oaxaca, Mexico. This tree, El Tule, is said to embody the love and unity of people who merge their hearts together and work to fulfill the teachings of the Creator.

As history has amply recorded, this emphasis on the heart was later distorted by the Aztecs in a ritual of bloody sacrifice. William Irwin Thompson expresses that distortion vividly in his book *Blue Jade from the Morning Star:* "In the religion of Quetzalcoatl, one learned . . . how to open one's heart to the light of the sun. The opening of the heart center to the light is one of the sublime religious experiences. . . . The Aztecs, however, perverted the ancient practice, reduced it to a fundamentalist literalism, and began to rip open the chests of sacrificial victims so that the priest could hold the heart up to the sun."

Despite this later perversion, the core of Quetzalcoatl's message was noble and highly advanced. This reality was ultimately obscured through the zealous work of missionaries, just as the merciful message of Jesus Christ was distorted by the Inquisition, the Ku Klux Klan, the Jonestown massacre, and other infamous episodes in the Christian dispensation.

Especially in Central America, Quetzalcoatl is often symbolized by wavy lines. The lines represent the energy of electricity—the pure energy of creative intelligence. This is also the meaning of the Feathered Serpent image. The serpent represents the Earth because it lives so close to the Earth and

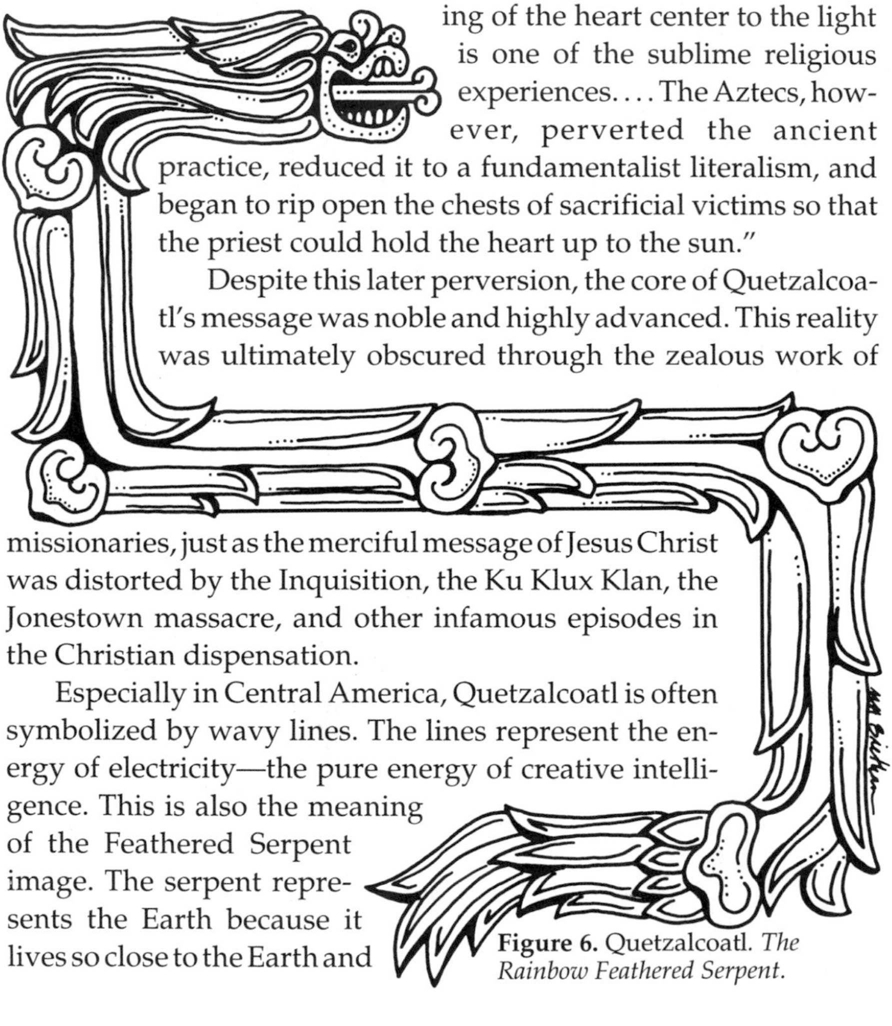

Figure 6. Quetzalcoatl. *The Rainbow Feathered Serpent.*

uses its whole being to go forward in life. The feathers, which are the feathers of an eagle, represent Spirit because the eagle, of all creatures, flies closest to the heavens. In the symbol of the Feathered Serpent, Earth and Spirit are therefore brought together and integrated in a good way, much as they are in the symbol of the rainbow. The rainbow suggests that all the colors and pathways of creation are to be respected and honored. Quetzalcoatl is said to be the embodiment of the serpent rainbow beam of cosmic intelligence—the electric sperm of the universe fertilizing the womb of the Earth.

Interestingly, the Central American symbol of the Feathered Serpent is strongly akin to the central healing symbol of Western medicine: a staff entwined by two serpents. Known as the caduceus or staff of Hermes, it is universally identified as the emblem of the modern physician.

Figure 7. The Caduceus, or Hermes' Staff. *The universal symbol of the medical profession.*

In his book *The Way of the Physician,* Dr. Jacob Needleman poses two provocative questions: Why is this symbol used, and where does it come from? "The staff of Hermes," he answers, "was one of the principal symbols of the work of self-perfection. The two serpents represent the two fundamental forces of universal nature—one moving outward, away from the Source, and the second moving back toward union with the Source.

"The world of nature was understood [in the time of the classical Greek civilization] as the stage where these two opposing forces constantly war with each other. Out of this warfare the whole of the created world arises through the mediation and reconciliation of a third movement symbolized by the figure of a dove resting atop the staff in between the heads of the serpents."

In many later representations of this symbol, Dr. Needleman points out, the dove is replaced by a pair of wings. In Christian terminology, this winged principle of reconciliation is known as the Holy Spirit or Holy Ghost.

The classical Greek symbol actually derives from the much more ancient wisdom of the Vedic tradition of India. In that tradition, the spiraling snakes represent the lunar and solar forces at work in the energy body of all human beings. The serpent force, seen as residing in the central channel or spinal cord, is the power of kundalini as it spirals up the body until the force reaches the crown of the head, from which the spirit takes flight.

Taken as a whole, the image of the physican's caduceus is strikingly similar to the Central American symbol of the Feathered Serpent. According to the prophecies of Turtle Island, now is the time when this similarity is becoming plain to those who will look.

When the World Seemed to Be Dying

Quetzalcoatl is said to have foretold many of the important events to occur in the thousand years following his death. In particular, he prophesied that he would return one day in the same manner that he left: over the eastern ocean. Before he returned, he said, bearded white men would come in boats with sails like white wings. They would conquer the Indians and force on them a different religion—a beautiful religion, but one that many white men would not live up to themselves.

Later, Quetzalcoatl prophesied, when the world seemed to be dying from abuses of the science brought by the light-skinned conquerers, the Tree of Life (El Tule) would wither and die, symbolizing the end of one age and the start of another. As understood by the Toltecs, our present world has been preceded by four other worlds or creations, all of which have been destroyed as they became spiritually corrupt—the last one by a great flood.

Quetzalcoatl also prophesied that after his passing the world would go through thirteen fifty-two-year cycles of increasing light and choice, followed by nine fifty-two-year cycles of increasing darkness and trouble: the Nine Hells. According to many students of the calendars that record this prophecy, the last of the Nine Hells came to an end on August 16, 1987. At that point, they say, we entered a twenty-five-year epoch of transition to the next phase of world evolution: the world of the Sixth Sun.

As Quetzalcoatl foresaw it, our fate during the time of transition will be, as ever, in our own hands. We can destroy the world through selfish thoughts and actions or we can come into harmony with divine order and all the creations of the Earth. We possess free will and thus can choose one or the other.

Crisis in Consciousness

In an unpublished manuscript entitled "Ancient Mexican Prophecy for the New Age," writer and researcher Eugene Johnson links the Central American prophecies to the persistent legend of Atlantis—a continent that, according to myth, was located in the middle of what we know today as the Atlantic Ocean.

Johnson believes Atlantis was the home port of Noah and other boat people who survived the great flood. This flood is remembered in more than two hundred cultures around the world—African, Australian, Native American, Tibetan and Chinese, as well as Greek and Jewish—as the event that destroyed the world before this one, the world of the Fourth Sun, in Aztec terminology. When Atlantis went under the ocean waves, those who were wise and good were said to have escaped in boats and eventually to have seeded the future civilizations of Europe, Egypt, Australia, the Orient, and the Americas. Johnson believes that ancient American cultures had a prophetic sense that their new world would one day also come to end. Their prophecies, he says, are encoded in the architecture of their Central American pyramids and in the mathematical symbols on their calendars.

Johnson writes that the city of Teotihuacan, a few miles northeast of Mexico City, served for centuries as the primary seat of learning and religious ceremony for the Americas. At its zenith around A.D. 600, it was probably the largest city in the world. The name Teotihuacan means "birthplace of the gods." According to legend, the city and its elegant pyramids were built at the beginning of the Aztec Fifth Sun, after the Atlantean cataclysm, to commemorate the start of that new age and to set forth in their design and proportions a prophecy of the spiritual plan for the generations to come.

Teotihuacan is said to be a power center, connected by ley lines (energy lines) to hundreds of other holy sites around the world such as Stonehenge, Chaco Canyon, Machu Picchu, Mount Katahdin, and the Egyptian pyramids. Johnson says Teotihuacan, with its mysterious ceremonial pyramids, served as a primary focal point for the subtle energies that infused the Earth during the summer of 1987.

No one knows for sure what the new world cycle will bring, according to Johnson. But in his manuscript he does indulge in some cautious speculation: "It's unreasonable to expect that suddenly, in 1987, the diseased conditions which plague the world will evaporate, leaving us in a blissful state of perfection. The world must go through a 'cleansing' of some sort to open up sufficient space for new development to begin."

The event of August 16, 1987, which came to be known as Harmonic Convergence, was said to have begun a twenty-five year cycle when subtle energy currents would be released, accelerated, and intensified to work in the world. The keynote for this prophetic period, Johnson suggests, is a crisis in consciousness, a period of intense spiritual action in the world and in the souls of the people.

In technical terms, using a related Mayan calendar, August 16, 1987, was the last day of the nineteenth katun of the thirteenth baktun. The dawn of August 17, 1987, was the beginning of the last part of the entire 5,125-year cycle depicted in one of seventeen Mayan calendars. In other words, according to this particular Native American system, August 16, 1987, marked the end of a cycle of Earth's history that began in 3113 B.C., and it initiated a brief transitional phase leading to the winter solstice of December 2011. By the Aztec system of reckoning, we are entering the world of the Sixth Sun; by the more widely accepted Hopi system of reckoning, we are entering the world of the Fifth Sun.

Harmonic Convergence

In his controversial book *The Mayan Factor: Path Beyond Technology*, poet and visionary José Argüelles, Ph.D., set out an elaborate interpretation of the events prophesied in Native American calendars. Argüelles wrote that since the beginning of what he calls the Mayan Great Cycle, we have been passing slowly through a beam of cosmic energy 5,125 years wide. The cosmic intention of that beam of energy, he wrote, has been to accelerate the vibratory rate of subtle energies on Earth and to bring them into harmony with the vast spiral of the Milky Way galaxy, of which our sun is part.

In the summer of 1987, Argüelles argued, we began a radical quickening of energy and consciousness that will last twenty-five years—until December 21, 2011. This is his interpretation of the final date in one of the prophetic Mayan calendar, though other sources give the end date as 2012, 2013, and 2026. At any rate, at that time, according to Argüelles, our galactic synchronization will be complete. Whatever parts of our civilization have survived the time of transition will be in harmony with the great spiral of the galaxy, a spiral evident in the winds, in the waters, and in all living forms on Earth—even in the spiral of DNA in human cells. Argüelles believes that by the end of the Native American calendar we will have found a path that allows us to go beyond the limits and perils of the machine age—a path that blends Spirit with technology, heaven with Earth.

One critical moment in this transition, Argüelles wrote, occurred at sunrise on the morning of Sunday, August 16, 1987. That moment began what he called Harmonic Convergence, the accelerated release of potent cosmic energies. Argüelles helped organize multimedia arts festivals around the world to celebrate this event and to create focal points for the arrival of the cosmic impulse.

According to Argüelles, from the moment of that August sunrise, the world began to undergo intensified transformative chaos, the climax of the disastrously corrupt materialism of the industrial world. This global chaos, he wrote in 1987, will include the collapse and regrouping of major governments, as well as deindustrialization and demilitarization. But, he added, "it is precisely at the climax of matter, the fateful moment of materialism's full ripenesss, that the highest and culminating purpose of the entire historical cycle will reveal itself." This new revelation, or paradigm, Argüelles said, will be a unified planetary consciousness, marked by an inspired and illumined humanity.

Ceremonial Time

Consider the context of the mythology and prophecies associated with Harmonic Convergence. Overlooked for many years, these prophecies came to the fore at a time when issues of Central American policy occupied a critical place in public consciousness— a time when Mexico and all of Central America were in great economic and social unrest. In combination with other world events, the scene appeared set for something dramatic to happen.

In the years just before Harmonic Convergence, the times were marked by some stunning happenstances. In the summer of 1985, for example, six Soviet cosmonauts shared an amazing encounter while they orbited the Earth in their *Salyut 7* space station. As reported widely in the Soviet press and in *Parade* magazine in the United States, the cosmonauts all observed a band of angels. "What we saw," reported a spokesperson for the six scientists, "were seven figures in the form of humans, but with wings and mistlike halos, as in the classic depiction of angels. Their faces were round with cherubic smiles." Twelve days later in their mission, they saw the angels a second time. Discounting skeptics' allegations that they experienced a mass hallucination, cosmonaut Svetlana Savitskaya reported, "The angels were smiling, as though they shared in a glorious secret."

Likewise, in April of 1986, the year before Harmonic Convergence, a tragedy of staggering proportions unfolded at the Chernobyl nuclear reactor in the Soviet Union—a tragedy that caught the world's attention. While commenting on the incident later in the *New York Times,* reporter Serge Schmemann told of his meeting with a prominent Russian writer who had produced a tattered old Bible, and, with a practiced hand, turned to the story of the Apocalypse. The writer encouraged the reporter to listen carefully to what he promised would be an incredible passage: "And the third angel sounded, and there fell a great star from heaven, burning as if it were a lamp, and it fell upon the third part of the rivers, and upon the fountains of waters; and the name of the star is called Wormwood; and many men died of the waters because they were made bitter." In a dictionary, the writer turned to the Ukrainian word for wormwood, a bitter wild herb used as a tonic in rural Russia. The reporter bent over and saw the word written plain: *Chernobyl.*

No doubt about it. By the time 1987 arrived, late in the millennium, the world was awash in anguish, greed, uncertainty, and hope. Powerful energies were already at work in the world. Whether they were taking cues from the nightly news, the Bible, the Sphinx, or outer space, most people already felt that we were living in a time of transition. But a transition to what?

No one will know for sure, of course, until we get wherever we're going. But at the time of Harmonic Convergence, many people on many paths—Rainbow Warriors—had already dedicated their lives to helping steer Planet Earth toward a higher destiny, a spiritual destiny. Therefore, thousands of people used the prophesied shift to a New Age—whether that shift was a real event or just a working hypothesis—to engage in spiritual action consecrated to healing the world.

A Turning Point

Shortly after the prophetic year of 1987 began, astronomers observed a rare and unsettling phenomenon in the skies over the Southern Hemisphere: a supernova, the explosive death of a star. According to scientists, in that spectacular explosion, a distant star released in a few seconds as much energy as our sun puts out in ten billion years. Supernova 1987a was the signal celestial event of a wild year, which peaked in a summer notable for stunning news.

The summer of 1987 was the summer when the five billionth baby was born on Planet Earth; the summer that used syringes and dead dolphins began washing up on shores; the summer the world debt grew beyond imagination; the summer Wall Street fed in an unfounded frenzy, gorging toward an October crash; the summer banks began to crumble; the summer AIDS and miniskirts were juxtaposed; the summer the ozone hole grew larger, the forests smaller, and the thirty-six wars more intense; the summer we learned that one-third of the Earth's water was polluted; the summer preachers became mired in petty failings; the summer Americans began shooting at each other on freeways.

Photo 10. Supernova 1987a. *An extremely rare celestial event, the explosion of a distant star, marked the early part of the year that Harmonic Convergence occurred. Astronomers said Supernova 1987a, visible only in the Southern Hemisphere, exploded 175,000 years ago; it took the light that long to reach Earth. Mythologists pondered the possible meaning of this omen. Photo by Marcelo Bass/National Optical Astronomy Observatories.*

In the summer of 1987, most people had a sense that we had reached a fateful turning point in our collective destiny. The only question was, which way would we turn? Pollster George Gallup, Jr., summed up the situtation in July when he told a Minnesota prayer breakfast that, based on his polls, most Americans felt we were facing "a moral and ethical crisis of the first dimension."

The summer of 1987 also brought word from ancient mystical sources that deliverance was at hand—that the dawning of the New Age was only a matter of weeks away. The news hit a sizable segment of the nation and world right in the heart. The prophecies were a laser beam of hope in a messy and murky world. After all, a lot of people had been waiting impatiently for something called the New Age since the 1960s. There was already a vast reservoir of pent-up frustration. In the context of the world's history, and in the jagged rhythm of the summer's news, was it at all surprising that there was such a rush to respond?

Harmonic Convergence had great romantic appeal. It promised to empower people acting out of love and strength to bring peace and harmony into the world. Most of the people who participated were not only sincere but also mature and skilled—in the arts and crafts, the sciences, the mysteries, and in all walks of life. The Flower Children and all their relations had done a lot of growing and learning since the Summer of Love in the late 1960s. Harmonic Convergence was a great excuse to express their deepest aspirations, to reconnect the Woodstock Nation, and to take action with the skills they had acquired.

José Argüelles, who helped popularize the event with his book, put it this way: "The world had been without vision for so long that Harmonic Convergence awakened in many different kinds of people a stirring in the breast, an ache in the heart, a recollection of ancient power and legendary meaning that had long been past."

As the summer built to a cresendo, thousands began to fervently believe that with purification and prayer they could make a difference in the fate of the world—that they could tip the scales in favor of an age of peace.

National Fruit Loops Day?

With a queer and unbecoming bitterness, Gary Trudeau, who came of age in the sixties, had the characters in his comic strip "Doonesbury" label August 16 the "Moronic Convergence—a sort of National Fruit Loops Day." Following his lead, much of the mass media fairly choked on hyperbole, cynicism, and inaccuracy as they reported on the buildup to the event. The criticisms had an oddly perverse twist, as if the critics believed there was nothing to believe in at all.

As the summer of 1987 wore on, Harmonic Convergence took on a life of its own, far bigger than any one prophecy, timetable, or spokesperson. Word raced from meditation group to newsletter to network. At Digital Equipment Corporation, for example, there were a reported 160 entries about the event on the in-house computer system. The word was out.

Was Harmonic Convergence just a wild-eyed New Age fantasy? Was it real but too subtle to perceive? Was everyone chasing after a false Christ? Or had the New Age begun to blossom at last? There are a thousand answers to these questions, none of them certain. But one thing is for sure: the date served as an effective focus for prayer around the world. Thousands upon thousands of people decided they didn't care whether anything cosmic was happening or not: they were going to make their prayers and then teach and support a way of life that would be at peace with the Earth and all the creations who share it. They were going to take action as Rainbow Warriors.

They Beat on Drums

While meteor showers creased the mid-August night, people sat and waited—alone, by the hundreds, by the thousands. They waited across North America, South America, and across the entire planet. That such a massive and far-flung gathering could have happened seemed improbable if not impossible at the start of summer 1987. But such was the combined power of the grapevine and the mass media that by mid-August many millions knew about Harmonic Convergence and had a chance to participate in it.

Ultimately, so bombastic was the ballyhoo that many people were waiting for UFOs to sweep down from the heavens, for extraterrestrials to dramatically materialize on Earth, and for celestial pyrotechnics on the order of Armageddon. Others were expecting more subtle but no less potent forces to work their way into the world.

Wherever the people were, when dawn came they beat on drums, they rang bells, they meditated on flowers, and they raised their voices in thanksgiving and prayer. They were the Harmonic Convergers, the Rainbow Warriors, and they made a strong prayer to start the blossoms unfolding in the Age of Flowers. They believed that ripples from their great prayer would start to spiral through an extensive network of people dedicated to healing the Earth.

Plenty to Spare

The participants in Harmonic Convergence were trying to reach a critical mass, to get the hundredth monkey in line at a sacred time and in a sacred place. The legends said it would take 144,000 people to reach this critical mass. Did enough people turn out?

According to Wendy Call, who worked at the Harmonic Convergence coordination office in Boulder, Colorado, in 1987, "Yes,

A Sampler of Harmonic Convergence Gatherings

Global Gatherings	*Number of Participants*
Great Pyramid, Egypt	1,500
Delphi, Greece	350
Reykjavik, Iceland	800
Eiffel Tower, Paris	400
Machu Picchu, Peru	100
Teotihuacan, Mexico	10,000
El Tule Tree, Oaxaca, Mexico	125
Ayer's Rock (Uluru), Australia	2,000
Mt. Warning (Wollombin), Australia	600
Sydney, Australia	3,000

Gatherings in the United States

Niagara Falls, NY	300
Colorado Springs, CO	500
Shelburne, VT	250
Enchanted Rock, TX	350
Redlands, CA	100
McCall, ID	300
Serpent Mound, OH	600
Stone Mountain, GA	100
Chaco Canyon, NM	3,000
Mount Shasta, CA	5,000
Fallsburg, NY	3,000
Mount Monadnock, NH	300
Cadillac Mountain, ME	800
Mount Wachusett, MA	200
Mystery Hill, Salem, NH	300
Bangor, ME	400
Haleakala Volcano, HI	5,000
Santa Barbara, CA	144
(outside Ronald Reagan's Western White House)	

Figure 8. A Sampler of Harmonic Convergence Gatherings. *This is just a small sampling. Thousands of other individuals and groups, large and small, gathered to contribute to the overall energy field created at Harmonic Convergence, August 16, 1987.*

with plenty to spare." She began her work in March, so she saw the event transform from a quiet plan for an art event to a mass-media global celebration. She said there were gatherings all over America and at sacred sites all over the world.

"There were hundreds and hundreds and hundreds of ceremonies," she said. "We have no way of verifying it, but we are certain that there were well over 144,000 people out there. From the calls and letters I saw, my general sense is that people had a wonderful time. It was a very good and positive experience. Many people report that they were surprised by the broad range of people involved—old, young, fat, thin, hippie, business, family, children—people from all walks of life."

Based on hundreds of individual reports, the experience of Harmonic Convergence appears to have been as diverse as the human community itself. Some greeted the sun with solemn meditation, others with drums and chanting or with crystals laid out in grids. Yet others greeted dawn at a Sun Dance, or with rock music and New Wave sunglasses as they watched the sky and Earth. Some few responded as if the event were a chance to lecture, or as if they were at a rock concert or a human circus. Most felt they were sharing sacred moments in sacred places. And then, inevitably, morning gave way to afternoon.

SIX

On the Threshold of Myth

With a wild flurry of media attention and feverishly inflated expectations, Harmonic Convergence had unfolded on mountain tops and at sacred sites around the world. Then it dropped from view, as if it had been a fantasy weekend and nothing more—as if that were all there had been to it.

However, many of those who greeted the dawn with prayers for peace and songs for the Earth, many who studied the ancient prophecies and the modern portents, say they saw something more. They say Harmonic Convergence was not a one-day event but rather the start of a brief, intense, twenty-five-year phase of evolution. They say that if we can move with the energy that was released, if we can bring it into our lives in a good way and honor all of creation, then the transition to a new time will be less traumatic, more harmonious.

Are they right? Was there a great mystical influx of energy? Did an ancient cycle of world history come to an end? Did the summer of 1987 mark a sharp acceleration in the rate of world change? In the years since Harmonic Convergence, there have been many dramatic world events. But can those events be correlated with Harmonic Convergence?

Even among students of prophecy, controversy has raged over whether Harmonic Convergence was a real event and whether José Argüelles and others correctly interpreted the ancient calendars of Turtle Island. About this controversy, Argüelles once responded, "As far as the dates on the calendar, it doesn't really matter whether

I was right or wrong. Something happened and something's happening. Just look around."

Just Looking Around

Many people reported seeing things at sunrise on August 16, 1987: rainbows, dragonflies, and clouds shaped like dragons. All of these are considered to be symbols of Quetzalcoatl, the Lord of the Dawn, the legendary Central American leader whose spirit is said to be connected to fulfillment of the calendar. As suggested in advance by many observers, thousands of people did in fact have profound dreams and visions during Harmonic Convergence. Some people also say they saw UFOs, specifically on Mount Shasta in California and at Teotihuacan in Mexico.

The year that followed Harmonic Convergence was marked by much disruption. Arabs and Israelis clashed on the ancient prophetic Temple Mount in Jerusalem. Sikhs and Hindus warred upon each other in the sacred Golden Temple of Amritsar in India. A group of

Photo 11. Harmonic Convergence at Niagara Falls. *As people marked Harmonic Convergence at Niagara Falls, they were greeted by a rainbow, a familiar phenomenon at the falls. Photo © 1987 by Robert Ford.*

machine-gun-toting fanatics attacked pilgrims in Mecca, setting off a bloody massacre at the time of the Haj, the sacred pilgrimage of the Muslim religion. In Tibet, normally pacific Buddhist monks came to believe that all of their ancient prophecies had been fulfilled, so in frustration they rioted violently in attempts to throw off Chinese domination and restore the Dalai Lama to authority.

Since the summer of 1987, the tone and undertone of world news has consistently conveyed the sense that we are living in ominously momentous times. On May 23, 1988, for example, CBS News reported that America's bird population was in dramatic decline and that we had immediate cause to fear a Silent Spring. "The birds," intoned Dan Rather, "are sending us a warning." The same might be said about the whales and dolphins washing up on the shores of our fouled oceans, about the dying forests, about the invasion of poinsettia whitefly on vegetable crops, and about our poisoned lakes, streams, and wells.

Now, in the early 1990s, the oceans of the world have begun to experience explosions of toxic algae blooms such as the red tides that have had catastrophic effects on fisheries and aquaculture; meanwhile, beds of sea grass are rapidly shrinking in many coastal areas around the world, eliminating a vital nursery for the marine species that are the foundation of the food chain. Many scientists have cautioned that these are early warning signs of massive ecological breakdown. As the immune system of the Earth is attacked and weakened, so, too, is the human immune system attacked and weakened by the poisons of industrial culture.

Storms bearing winds of one hundred and forty miles per hour and more have slammed England, France, Japan, Bangladesh, and the Philippines; unusually high winds have also ripped through Australia and the heartland of America. According to the U.S. Geological Survey, 1987 was a near-record year for earthquakes. Since then, earthquakes and other natural disasters have continued to rattle the planet with increasing regularity. Volcanoes have flared to life. The protective layer of ozone has dissolved at a frightening pace, increasing the incidence of skin cancer and weakening the plants that feed humans and animals. Evidence suppporting the likelihood of the greenhouse effect has mounted, as has conflicting evidence that the world is cooling. Famine has returned with a vengeance to Africa, and general environmental deterioration has continued around the globe at a heart-sickening pace.

So sorry has been the state of the world that the Kogi have come forward. The Kogi are an indigenous group of people who live on Sierra Nevada de Santa Marta, the highest seaside mountain in the world, set dramatically on the shore of the Carribean Sea in Columbia. Having retreated to the remotest parts of the mountain four hundred years ago, the Kogi are said to be the only native civilization in South America not demolished by the Europeans who settled the area.

In the early 1990s, the Kogi, a deeply spiritual people who call themselves "The Elder Brothers," allowed a British Broadcasting Company (BBC) reporter to visit them, the first and last such visit they have ever allowed. They admitted the reporter and a cameraman because they had an urgent message they wished to deliver to the world, a message for their "younger brothers." The BBC film shows the sophisticated and harmonious culture the Kogi have maintained for centuries and then portrays several of the elders speaking their message. That messsage was shown on BBC in Britain, and then in America in 1991 on the Public Broadcasting System (PBS).

"We look after nature," the elders said, "and we see that you are killing it by what you do. We are asking you to stop. We can no longer repair the world. You must. We are here to give a warning to all the younger brothers and to all the world. You are taking out the Mother's heart and cuttting her up when you dig for the gold and all the minerals. Remember the Mother; she is the mind inside all of nature and also fertility and growth. We see the Earth is dying and losing her strength because of this. The water down below is drying up. When she dies, you will die. We don't know when the world will end, but it will end soon if you go on this way."

Transformational Themes

In the years since Harmonic Convergence, the onslaught of global change has been staggering. Political and economic upheaval has visited the Soviet Union, China, Africa, Iraq, Central America, Europe, and the Middle East. The banks, the insurance companies, and the corporations all have been rocked to their foundations by the forces at work in the world. They have been forced to restructure. Change has not, however, been limited to human institutions. Consider the following snippets from the realm of science:

- In 1988, anthropologists discovered human fossils in the Qafez Cave in Israel that they dated using a technique called thermoluminescence (heat and light). Previously, most scientists had thought humanity (Homo sapiens) was no more than 40,000 years old. The fossils proved that we've been here at least 100,000 years. In 1991, scientists discovered other fossils at Lake Baringo in Kenya that extended by 500,000 years the age of the genus Homo, the genus that includes modern humans. Previously, the earliest known Homo fossil was dated at 1.9 million years. The newly discovered fossils push the date back to about 2.5 million years. These findings have forced anthropologists to recast their theories of evolution.

- The most widely accepted theories about the age of the Earth peg it at about 4.5 to 4.6 billion years. But in the spring of 1988, Japanese planetologists discovered ten diamonds (crystals) in Zaire, Africa, that are at least six billion years old.

- For decades, scientists contended that North America had only been inhabited by human beings for the past 12,000 years—since the last Ice Age subsided. But in the spring of 1991, archaeologists digging in a cave at Orogrande, New Mexico, found convincing evidence—fire circles and spear points—that humans have lived on this continent for at least the last 35,000 years. This discovery is prompting a complete revision of American prehistory and buttressing the statements of Native American elders, who have long claimed that their ancestors have lived on this land for many, many thousands of years.

- The Torus project heated gases to a record temperature of two hundred million degrees Fahrenheit, which is almost ten times hotter than the sun. Scientists from fourteen European nations cooperated in the experiment, which was designed to replicate the complex process that takes place in the sun's core. This process, it is hoped, can someday be used to generate electricity.

✒ Columbia University began a systematic search of the Milky Way by activating the Very Large Array radio telescope. Scientists hoped to piece together a comprehensive picture of our home galaxy and thereby place the sun rightly in the context of the four hundred billion other stars that make up the giant spiral of the Milky Way.

✒ Japanese researchers discovered evidence that the heart of our Milky Way galaxy is in fact a huge black hole that spews out a magnetic tornado of energy seventy-five million billion miles long. This spiraling maelstrom of intense magnetic en-

Photo 12. M81. A typical spiral galaxy of about 400 million stars in the constellation Ursa Major (the Great Bear, or Big Dipper). The galaxy is said to be similar to the Milky Way, the home galaxy of our sun and planet Earth. As astronomer Carl Sagan once memorably put it, there are "billions and billions of galaxies in our universe." Photo by National Optical Astronomy Observatories.

ergy, the researchers said, bends and waves like a hose on a plane perpendicular to the relatively flat spiral of the galaxy.

✦ The National Geographic Society changed the official map of the world. The map in use for most of the last century wildly distorted the proportions of countries far from the equator, causing the Soviet Union to appear twice as large as it is in reality and the oceans to appear much smaller than they really are. Cartographers said the new map would give human beings a far more realistic view of their planet.

To these developments could be added major breakthroughs in superconductivity, nuclear fusion, and efforts to unravel the genetic code. Researchers even demolished a cherished myth by discovering two identical snowflakes.

Mythology of the Transition

In the mythology of Harmonic Convergence, one of the central themes is the expansion of human consciousness. José Argüelles said that, over the twenty-five years of transition, human consciousness would have the opportunity to expand from the relatively narrow confines of our solar system to the more universal perspective of the galaxy. Many of the developments since the summer of 1987 have indeed tended to erode the narrow confines of traditional beliefs. For example:

✦ Officials of the Roman Catholic church announced in 1988 that, after subjecting it to the scientific radiocarbon-dating process, they had concluded that the Shroud of Turin was a fake. The announcement undermined the faith of millions of people in a major religious talisman.

✦ An official group of Protestant and Catholic scholars concluded that Jesus was not, in fact, the author of the Lord's Prayer, as the gospels proclaim. This prayer, the foundational petition of Christians to God the Father, was instead ascribed to an earlier Hebrew teacher identified only as "Q." Then David Rosenberg and Harold Bloom sent shock waves through the literate world when they published *Book of J*. In that work, the two researchers showed that the predomin-ant narrative strand running through Genesis, Exodus, and Numbers is a composite of earlier literary sources. These composite chapters were assembled by a writer they identi-fy as "J." In all likelihood, this first author of the Bible was a woman.

Ireland's fiery Protestant minister Ian Paisley shocked the world community when he disrupted the address of Pope John Paul II to the European Parliament in 1988. The pope had barely begun his speech when the Reverend Paisley rose with a red poster in hand and loudly denounced the Holy Father as "the Antichrist."

In America and elsewhere around the world, people began a fundamental reassessment of recent history beginning with the arrival of Columbus in the New World. For the first time, evidence became widely available that Columbus's reign over Hispaniola (the island of modern-day Haiti and the Dominican Republic) had been an unmitigated horror. In the years immediately following 1492, his harsh policies and practices led directly to the extermination of the native popu-lation from Hispaniola (an estimated 125,000 to 500,000 hu-man beings). The actions of Columbus set a pattern that was continued in large measure by the explorers and settlers who followed him.

The Vatican ordered Dominican priest and scholar Matthew Fox to remain silent for one year because of his "heretical" teaching that "women and men must give birth to a creation-centered religious vision" that views the Earth and the body as sacred. Fox had preached that the Church's unbending emphasis on human sin had blinded it to travesties such as genocide and the rape of the Earth. He overturned the tra-ditional doctrine of "original sin" and replaced it with the concept of the fundamental human state as one of "original blessing."

The late 1980s and early 1990s were characterized by a sharp increase in UFO sightings, including dozens by reliable authorities from the military, the law, and science. One knowledgeable observer commented that the evidence had mounted so high that UFO news should be on page 1 of the newspapers, not back with the comics.

Mysterious crop circles began to appear with increasing frequency in the grain fields of England and in many other nations, including the United States. In 1991, two artists claimed responsibility for the circles, but their assertion that they had created all the circles as a hoax failed to convince careful observers. How, skeptics of their claim wondered, could two men with hand tools have created as many as seven hundred huge, meticulously laid-out geometrical patterns each summer, on several continents, without leaving footprints and without breaking a stalk of grain? Consequently, for many, the crop circles remained an unexplained mystery.

This list could be expanded to include yet other developments that are dramatically changing public perception of the way things are. Altogether, the changes appear to suggest a pattern in keeping with the theme of Harmonic Convergence: radical change in our world and in our relationship to the universe.

Campaign for the Earth

All this and much more has come to pass since Harmonic Convergence. Was Harmonic Convergence therefore a real cosmic event? Are we consequently in the midst of a complete global transformation? At this late stage of the millennium, when claims and counterclaims beset us from every side, it seems ill advised to grasp too quickly at pat explanations. So often, they are illusions. Yet the tone, pattern, and force of world events calls out for careful consideration. What is going on here?

In his book *The Mayan Factor: Path Beyond Technology*, José Argüelles wrote that, based on his study of the Amerindian cultures, he believed that after August 16, 1987, the currents of world events would combine to create a cresting wave of world history. He said there would be a shift in energy frequency at Harmonic Convergence, and that after that point the institutions and structures that were not in harmony with the circles and spirals of the emerging world would be shaken. The storm of transformation, he predicted, would likely intensify.

Argüelles suggested that the time we are living in should be thought of not so much as a time of destruction but rather as the Campaign for the Earth—an opportunity to change the world by bringing forward alternative ways of life that are in harmony with nature. He urged people to take the energy of the epoch and use it creatively, not just for themselves, but for the community of life. This, he felt, is the mandate of the Rainbow Warriors.

There Is Truth in This

In most Native American cosmologies, there is a belief that civilizations have existed on Earth many times before. They have been destroyed primarily because they developed technology and then employed it without wisdom. Around the globe, many traditional elders say we are obviously again in a period when technology dominates life and is generally being applied without wisdom.

Don Alejandro Cirilo Perez is president of the Maya Elders Council in Guatemala and a widely respected daykeeper, charged with keeping the prophecies and dreams of his people, as well as with keeping time according to the intricate mathematics of the Mayan calendars.

A warm man who is noted for his generosity of spirit, don Alejandro says the event called Harmonic Convergence did mark an important turning point according to the tradition of the Mayan calendars. "There is truth in the prophecies about the rainbow and

Photo 13. Don Alejandro Cirilo Perez. *Author photo.*

the rainbow people," don Alejandro says. "People from all of the Americas will unite with people from all the other nations, and they will realize that we are all family, brothers and sisters. This is not my personal vision, but a cosmic vision presented by all the elders—a vision that we all share.

"Big changes are coming in this frame of time. That's why it's important to talk now and tell people to respect Mother Earth, and to stop destroying the water, air, and mountains. We must respect all the creations of the Creator, and stop making those kinds of technologies that affect the solar rays that come to us on Earth. True scientists must think of our children. Care for each other; love each other without discrimination. That is my main message.

"We are in times of big changes for the Earth, big earthquakes and hurricanes, also big conflicts in politics and war. They [politicians] promise changes. But we know that at their big meetings, done in the name of making things better, they do not make changes that work. It's the same old thing. The people must make the changes themselves."

You Can See It, But You Have to Look

Although many native teachers believe that we are moving into a new epoch of history, their understandings of this transition are varied. Some say we are moving from the Fourth World to the Fifth World, and others say we are going from the Fifth World to the Sixth World. Ultimately, these distinctions are of small consequence. What emerges as universal and important is the theme of pervading change and the opportunities that result from that understanding.

One of the most articulate spokespeople for this time of transition is Yehwehnode, also called Two Wolves or She Whose Voice Rides on the Wind. More widely, she is known as Grandmother Twylah Nitsch of the Seneca Nation, founder of the Wolf Clan Teaching Lodge. She believes we are moving from the Fourth World to the Fifth World, and she has much to share on this theme.

Photo 14. Grandmother Twylah Nitsch. *Photo by Steven Schoff* © 1987.

Grandmother Twylah first heard her family's prophecies of the Earth cleansing when she was just ten years old. If people lost their spiritual values, the prophecies warned, the Earth would be cleansed. The prophecies made a deep impression on her. "There have been a series of worlds," she explains. "The first time the sun cleansed the Earth, next the moon did, then water. The fourth time, this time, the Earth will be cleansed by all of these forces. Those prophecies also foretold that a band of people would come to this continent from the East. They wouldn't know who they were or what their future held. They would seek answers by digging into the Earth, water, and Moon—lacking any understanding about these powers. When they began digging into the secrets of the sun [nuclear fission and fusion], the prophecies say, it would create the next cleansing.

"Most people only know about the Third World, Atlantis, which was cleansed by the great flood. But altogether there are seven worlds in the history of the Earth. From the First World," Twylah explains, "we inherited the gift of beauty. From the Second World, we inherited family structure, thus learning about the balance between physical and spiritual energy. From the Third World, we inherited clarity of purpose through self-discipline. In the Fourth World, we developed diversity of wisdom. The Fourth World, though, also spawned the syndrome of separation and control, creating wars and religions. We have now entered the time of the Fifth World, which began at Harmonic Convergence.

"North America and South America were the site of the First World. While we are now over the threshold of the Fifth World, there are obviously many hangovers still around from the Fourth World. In the Fourth World, the greatest division came when humankind became impatient and created a God—'Him'—out there somewhere, separate from men and women. We are not separate. But this had to happen in the history of the Earth. There were lessons that we needed to learn through this experience.

"When we honor the Great Mystery, we are at peace. There's a certain blindness now. People have their eyes closed. It's a disease. People say, 'Well, the world's a mess, but as long as it's not depriving me of food and shelter, I really don't need to do anything about it.' Yet we do need to make deep personal decisions about this. Some people choose not to see, to be blind, not to be responsible.

"In the Fifth World, illumination will be the central theme. Spiritual awareness will be common. Illumination radiates from the center. The focus is on truth—all the knowledge in the world is useless without it. We humans have to be willing to take a chance. What is wisdom? It's an inner knowing of truth, without a shadow of a doubt. But it can't stand alone; it's tied to the other qualities on the Medicine Wheel. This life is not a game but is based on the wisdom of the trees, the grasses, the stones, and all of life. Wisdom is also having a dream. If you have no dream, you can't tap into wisdom. If a person has an idea that flashes into their mind, that's the beginning of a dream. But they must bring life into the idea and develop the dream or it will pass on.

"Illumination is coming in the Fifth World," Grandmother Twylah asserts. "Any time there is a drastic change, it takes the environment and the people within the environment about twenty-five years to have this transition occur—to have the trend really felt and appreciated by the people. So if trees are burned down, for example, and then new ones are seeded, it's going to take about twenty-five years, if they're untouched, before some of them will look like trees again. So it will take some time before we see the full influence of the illumination of the Fifth World. It's happening, and you can see it, but you have to look."

SEVEN

The Message of the Hopi

While he was alive, Grandfather David Monongye of the Hopi people taught a simple but powerful lesson, not only to his adopted granddaughter Oh Shinnah, but to all who would listen. He told people, "We are all brothers and sisters. We are all flowers in Great Spirit's garden, and we share a common root. We have different gifts and colors, but we all share a root in the Earth Mother." Grandfather David was one of many wise and gentle Hopi elders.

Living on isolated and arid mesas in the part of Turtle Island now known as Arizona, the traditional Hopi have a religion that is at once both simple and elaborate. To a large degree, these Native Americans, whose name means "peaceful people," are guided by prophecy—prophecy that is now widely known around the world. Following what they believe are the original instructions of the Creator, they have lived plainly and respectfully for thousands of years in the desert. Although they are few in number and are lacking in what the modern world would call technological sophistication, many of their elders believe the Hopi play a critical role in the destiny of the world.

To understand this, one must first understand one of their foundational teachings. The Hopi believe that after a great flood destroyed the world before this one, the Creator appointed them guardians of certain sacred land. At that time, they say, the Creator gave them specific spiritual wisdom, along with some rocks bearing symbols depicting the way the future was likely to unfold. These rocks are known as the Hopi Prophecy Rocks.

Though there are disagreements concerning the exact interpretation of the symbols, many Hopi elders agree that for hundreds of years world events have been unfolding as described by the Hopi Prophecy Rocks. In our times—as prophesied in the rock symbols—the world seems to be in a phase known as *koyaanisqatsi*, chaos, the next great test of human beings. This is the Great Purification that completes the transition to a new era, a rainbow era known to the Hopi as the world of the Fifth Sun.

Figure 9. Kokopelli. *Hopi spirit of fertility and playfulness.*

As with the myths of Australian Aborigines and many other tribal cultures around the world, Hopi legend holds that in ancient days the rainbow of humanity was whole. All the people—red, white, black, and yellow—at one time recognized each other as brothers and sisters. Eventually, events forced them to part ways, but they all pledged that when they were reunited they would clasp hands again in a sacred handshake. Then all the brothers and sisters would work in harmony to bring together the material and spiritual aspects of the world. They would correct each others' faults and eventually live together again, side by side in fulfillment. The legends even specified the time when and place where the reunion would occur.

In 1519, in keeping with Hopi prophecy, light-skinned brothers arrived in their homeland, the place now called Arizona. Pedro de Tovar, a Spanish explorer, and a troop of seventeen conquistadors encountered the Hopi on a mesa not far from the village of Oraibi. The leader of the Hopi Bear Clan, who had gone out to meet the long-lost brothers, held out his hand, palm up, in the sign of greeting specified by the Hopi Prophecy Rocks. Thinking that the Indian was seeking a gift, de Tovar dropped some trinkets into his hand rather than clasping it in brotherhood. With this exchange, many Hopi began to believe that their light-skinned relations had forgotten the ancient pledge.

From the Hopi perspective, the ramifications of this lapse of memory were not long in coming. Based on their prophecies, the Hopi believed that, if things began to unfold in this way, there would come a day when they would be forced to develop the land under the dictates of a new ruler. For thousands of years, they had held their land in a communal and religious way, sharing all resources and making ceremonies to help hold the Earth in balance.

Their prophecies proved accurate when, in the late nineteenth century, Senator Henry L. Dawes of Massachusetts argued that the Red Nations would never progress as they were, for communal sharing involved no self-interest and no profit incentive. Thus, in 1890, Congress passed the Dawes Act, which allotted a portion of land to each individual on a reservation. Greed, jealousy, and separatism soon invaded the Hopi tribal lands. A system that had worked and supported its peoples for generation upon generation came to an end; the new system cast many Hopi into a material and spiritual poverty, the likes of which they could never have previously imagined.

Signs They Watched For

Traditional Hopi elders, who are responsible for guiding their people and maintaining their spiritual balance, believe that the world is perilously out of balance and that humanity is being tested again—just as we were tested in the world before this one, the world that was eventually purified by water through a great flood.

The Hopi Prophecy Rocks have given the elders signs to watch for: the rocks predicted the First World War, the Second World War, and then a "gourd of ashes poured from the sky," a metaphor most observers have correlated with the dropping of the atomic bombs at the end of World War II. Just as the world before this one need not have been destroyed by water if the people had heeded the warnings, the world today need not be purified by the prophesied four elements: earth, fire, wind, and water. According to Hopi elder Thomas Banyacya, the Hopi believe that the people of the Earth have the opportunity and the responsibility to avoid this fate. But each person and each nation must ask whether they are contibuting to the imminent destruction of the Earth, either through misguided action or indifference. And then things must be set straight.

The Hopi were given specific instructions by way of their prophecy rocks. They were told that, when the modern world came to a time of great imbalance, they were to make four attempts to address the leaders of the world in "a House of Mica" that would one day stand on the eastern shore of this land. That House of Mica, the Hopi believe, is the United Nations, housed in a New York City building with a distinctive glass facade.

If the Hopi are recognized and permitted to speak, they can reveal some of their secret spiritual knowledge and thereby help the people of the world rediscover and realign themselves with the original instructions of the Creator. These instructions likely include the traditional Native American understanding that we exist in a universe of living spirit, that all things are sacred and related, and that respect and harmony must prevail.

In this latter part of the twentieth century, many people have written letters, lobbied, and demonstrated to help the Hopi gain recognition before the United Nations. The United States government, however, has vigorously opposed all attempts to have the Hopi recognized. Although accounts vary, many people believe that by October 1991, Hopi elders had completed their prophesied obligation by making four attempts to address the General Assembly of the United Nations. As of this writing, they were not permitted to speak.

The Stone Tablets

On December 13, 1990, two Hopi elders, greatly concerned about the events unfolding in the Persian Gulf before the start of the battle known as Desert Storm, made a pilgrimage to Santa Fe, New Mexico. There they warned that humankind must return immediately to peaceful, Earth-honoring ways or the world would soon come to a catastrophic end.

According to a report in the *Albuquerque Journal*, the Hopi elders made their appeal in Santa Fe because it was the first European capital among the Indian people, founded in 1610, and thus had special significance for them.

At the meeting, the elders said that the Earth was getting "close to its last stages." They said the prophecy rocks have instructed the Hopi to watch for signs that the world is on a dangerous course. The final stage of this dangerous course, they said, can be identified by famine, sickness, earthquakes, natural disasters, and, finally, by the dangerous buildup of weapons that "are destructive to all mankind." Referring generally to "events around the world," elder Thomas Banyacya said, "We are getting around to a dangerous period of our lives."

The sacred stones are said to have been given to the Hopi people by Maasaw, the Great Spirit, when the Hopi people emerged from hiding places within the Earth at the start of the Fourth World. According to the Hopi, there are other people around the world who were also were given stones by the Great Spirit. If the people all come together and follow the original instructions on these stones, the world can move through the purification consciously, with minimal tumult and destruction.

The Final Stage of the Prophecies

The Santa Fe pilgrimage of Thomas Banyacya and the other Hopi elder caused great controversy among some of the Hopi people because the two acted independently rather than with the full agreement of the Hopi Nation. Still, their statements carried a powerful message.

The text of their statement was reprinted in the midwinter 1991 edition of *Akwesasne Notes*, the official publication of the Mohawk Nation. A portion of that text follows.

> The stone tablets represent our ancient title to this land, which has existed for many centuries before the arrival of Columbus, and has never been relinquished to this day. They have been entrusted to us under the highest authority, to be held until the last stage of our prophecies has been completed. The signs that we have entered that final stage are now clear.
>
> In fulfillment of our spiritual instructions, we have come to Santa Fe, the oldest European capital on our land, to offer the people of the United States of America, and all humanity, a final

chance to collaborate with the forces of creation to purify our lives and restore peace to the world. . . .

Maasaw is both a real person and a manifestation of the Creator. We met him in person near the place where we built our mother village of Oraibi after a long migration to claim the land in his name. At that point he gave us permission to live here as caretakers, as well as the spiritual knowledge [*potskwani*] by which to keep the forces of life in balance. This knowledge is implanted in our sacred stone tablets.

But when the Europeans came, they forced their foreign religions, culture, and language upon our children, which brought great division among our people. As a result, today our young people are turning away from the basic law. They no longer understand it. They only understand the white man's law.

The elders said that because foreign religions, culture, and language have been forced upon the Indian children, "there is now hardly anyone fulfilling the sacred instructions and correctly performing the ceremonies essential to the Hopi way of life. There are still leaders from various clans who know of these instructions, which reveal their true purpose in life, but more and more they are turning away. This intrusion by outside forces, and the harmful effect on our function as caretakers of life, is the reason life on Earth is now so disturbed."

Planting a Seed of Realization

As they stood before the meeting, the elders said that each Hopi clan has a special function by which it helps hold life in balance. The Hopi clans were still carrying out their functions when the Europeans arrived. "We know these foreigners once had similar spiritual means for promoting life, with which they were supposed to bless the native peoples. But they had apparently misused their power. Most of the native people were forcibly stripped of their culture, language, and religious ceremonies, depriving them of their function as caretakers.

"[For these reasons] we bring our sacred stone tablets to the

New Mexico state capital in Santa Fe. . . . The Spanish, the Mexican, and the United States governments have all fought over someone else's land without consulting the original native peoples living on it, then created some kind of document to 'prove' their ownership. But what of the rights of the original native peoples? Who has the ability to look into this and see that the basic rights of the Hopi and other native people are restored?

"This is the key to the problem that threatens all life on Earth. If someone can uncover this information and bring it before the world, it might be possible to reverse the destruction of the native cultures that lies at the root of the destruction that now threatens our entire world."

In the 1990 book *Native American Prophecies*, journalist Scott Peterson interviewed a Hopi elder of the One Horn Society in Hotevilla, Arizona, who offered his insight on the issue of land title: "The ultimate philosophical foundation for the cultural values that exist in Hopi culture is that nobody owns the land. You have the right to use it. If you have the energy, the motivation, and the ability to provide the necessary food or whatever from working this Earth, and take care of it, you have the right to use it. That's all. You can't claim this acre is yours, or that two acres.

"The stone tablets only really mean that this is a path of life and instruction for people to exist with the elements on the Earth. If you interpret it this way, that tablet only means that whenever people get together and figure out a way to establish a situation where they can live in harmony, then the path will have been followed."

At the 1990 meeting in Santa Fe, in addition to speaking about the human relationship with the land, the two Hopi elders made several other telling points: "The great powers of the modern world need to realize that if they are to escape the punishment that lies ahead, what they are doing to native peoples around the world must be corrected. Those who accumulated power at the expense of the native peoples think they have a God-given right, but in doing so they are increasing the threat to all life. And although they now recognize that threat, they are powerless to reverse it by any means unless they stop preying upon the native peoples.

"We came here to plant the seed of this realization, which could turn the course of all humanity away from disaster. . . . Because our true original land title is essential to our role in holding this land and life in balance, we have never compromised that title by signing a treaty with the United States government. We have never given it authority to destroy our culture and take our land, nor have the other original native peoples. Yet this is being done here and throughout the world. . . .

"They are cutting our land into small allotments, confiscating our livestock, and allowing the land to be stripped of its mineral resources. Underground water is being depleted and the land is drying up. Open-pit uranium mines are polluting the area with radioactivity, causing the birth of many deformed babies. This shows what is happening to indigenous people around the world. . . .

"But as the Great Purification foretold in our tradition materializes, [the abusers] will get kicked around. They will find themselves disrespected everywhere, just as they have disrespected others, and their power will collapse. Soon they will see how little power and authority they really have.

"We hope they will heed our warning for their own sake, and for the sake of the native peoples who want nothing more than to rule themselves peacefully without being dictated to by anyone else. Part of the commission we received from the Creator through Maasaw is to sound this warning to the world. . . .

"We Hopi know our true white brother is to come and help us. He has a stone tablet representing his own title and power within the Creator's plan. By placing it together with our stone tablets, he may call upon the natural forces to purify the world. If the task of purification is left to these natural forces, we may be all wiped out. So it is up to all people to purify themselves voluntarily."

Calling the World's Attention

At the Santa Fe meeting, which included Bruce King, the governor of New Mexico, the independent Hopi elders also made a statement that rings with authority when we consider the plight of the Kurdish people after the destruction of Desert Storm in the

Middle East. "The deployment of armies to [allegedly] protect the freedom of native peoples abroad is causing the loss of that very freedom. It is the task of the Hopi to warn everyone concerned that, even though done in the name of freedom, this will unquestionably lead to a Third World War much worse than the first two, which may leave hardly any life on Earth. . . .

"The severe problems that face not only humanity, but every form of life on Earth, serve to warn that the time of destruction is at hand. That is why we act now to call world attention to the true nature of aboriginal land title, which alone holds the key to world peace. Hopi land title is based on our agreement with the Creator, the true owner of the land, through our meeting with Maasaw, to serve as its caretakers. This requires genuine knowledge of the pattern through which people can live together in peace without relying on the use of force. This way of life can continue forever."

The Return of Pahana

According to Robert Boissière's 1990 book, *The Return of Pahana: A Hopi Myth*, Pahana or Bahana is the name given by the Hopi to the mythic brother of an original pair of twins whose role was to insure harmony in the world. Pahana, who was of white coloration (the word also means "white man"), decided to leave the original people to investigate the rest of the world. He headed east. As a sort of passport, he took with him portions of an original stone tablet that had been given to the Hopi by Maasaw, the god-guardian of Earth.

To this day, Boissière writes, most Hopi believe neither Pahana nor the tablet have returned. However, Hopi myth predicts that Pahana will return bearing the other stone tablet when his power is needed to reestablish balance and harmony in the world. Furthermore, the Hopi believe that this time is imminent, just as fundamentalist Christians believe the Second Coming is imminent:

"Of all the Mesoamerican myths that have resurfaced from the past, the Quetzalcoatl-Pahana myth of the returning savior is the most widely recognized. It not only underlies the entire esoteric and mystic past of native America, but it is also astonishingly similar to the Old World myth of the Second Coming, which had its sources in

Chaldean, Sumerian, Babylonian, Assyrian, Greek, Egyptian, and Roman mythology."

Boissière concludes his discussion of Pahana with an assessment many others have also made: "Considering such sources as the Bible, Nostradamus, and Toltec, Zapotec, Chichimec, Mayan, and Incan texts, as well as current world events, I think it is reasonable to say that the Second Coming—the transformation of the planet through the Christ energy—will occur gradually during the last part of this century and the early part of the next. In other words, we are in the 'last days' right now, though many are too blind to recognize this fact."

EIGHT

Seeing the Rainbow from Down Under: The Tales of Alinta

*F*rom her home in Australia, Lorraine Mafi-Williams has journeyed to America and around the world. Known also as Alinta—Woman of the Fire—Lorraine tells the Aboriginal stories that are the heritage of Australia, the Land of the Everlasting Spirit. She also tells stories of the ancient linkages between Australia and America, linkages that she says will play a critical part in the reemergence of the rainbow.

Lorraine says a central part of her life mission is to help reestablish the legendary and critical link between the Aborigines of Australia and the American Indians of Turtle Island. She tells her tales with strong, expressive eyes, captivating turns of language, and film.

"I was born beside a freshwater spring on the outskirts of Purfleet Mission at Taree," Lorraine explains. "It was on the eighth of August, 1940, at dawn. They tell me I was the last baby to be born in the traditional way. My mother was accompanied by her aunt and the midwife. That day, a white crane came to feed in the water nearby. The old women said this was a good omen.

"My mother was a traditional medicine woman and healer, and my father was a linguist. His job was to teach and pass on the many dialects associated with the north coast tribes of New South Wales. He was also an initiated man, having learned the rules and lore of his tribe, the Bundjalung of Lismore. My mother was a Thungutti woman, whose ancestors originated west of the Blue Mountains."

As a child, Lorraine was a victim of the "stolen generation" of

Photo 15. Alinta (Lorraine Mafi-Williams). *Photo by Matthew Tung.*

Aborigines—children the government ordered removed from the care of their parents and put to work in white households. Pressed into domestic service, Lorraine did not see her parents from age twelve until nearly her twentieth birthday. Then her education in the rich tradition of the Aborigine people began in earnest.

"I was taken back to the Dreamtime teachings by the old people, beginning with the Githrabaul tribe, where I met and eventually married a Githrabaul man. Starting with my father-in-law and his mother, I was told many things of a deep cultural and spiritual nature, and I was initiated in these teachings. The Dreamtime is the source of both past reality and future possibilities."

Throughout her adult life, Lorraine has also been trained by Mrs. Millie Boyd. Known widely as Aunt Millie, she is an elder of the Githrabaul people, a clan of the Bundjalung tribe, whose ancestral territory is along the north coast of New South Wales. Aunt Millie is a "clever woman"—a shaman and medicine woman trained in the old ways of the Aborigines. She is the traditional custodian of Mount Warning (Wollombin) and also of Nimbin Rocks, Tooloom Falls, and Crown Mountain.

Wollombin is a sacred mountain, the first place that the sun touches in Australia each morning. Aboriginal people believe that the mountain absorbs the rays of the sun, which activate a large rose-quartz crystal hidden in its depths. In turn, the crystal is said to send the rays to Ayer's Rock, or Uluru, which then transmits these rays to Tibet.

Just as Native Americans have ancient and profound ties to the people of Tibet, so do the Aborigines. In fact, all three are linked: the Tibetans, the Native Americans, and the Australian Aborigines.

According to an ancient Tibetan Buddhist prophecy, the Aborigines and Tibetans would come together again when the balance of the world was threatened by greed—when it was time to make the transition to a New Age. The prophecy stated that an era would come when the sacred teachings would be suppressed inside Tibet, as has happened since China invaded that small nation in the late 1950s. The Tibetans would then reappear in a southern land with a great red rock at its center. Since the early 1980s, Tibetan lamas, including Lama Zazep Tulka, have been making pilgrimages to the massive red rock at the heart of Australia: Ayer's Rock, or Uluru. There they join in prayers and ceremony.

Aunt Millie, who had attained the age of ninety-six in 1991, is especially privy to this three-part relationship, for she is the keeper of Wollombin, the sacred mountain believed to be the home of the Native American spirit Waugatha. Some years ago, Aunt Millie delegated Lorraine as her "liaison officer" to the outside world. In a show of Aboriginal protocol, Aunt Millie never talks directly of the most sensitive spiritual matters. She talks to Lorraine, and Lorraine passes on the information.

Lorraine's teachings embrace all of the traditional Aboriginal lore. Her tribal name, Alinta, or Woman of the Fire, was given to her because she has been trained in what she calls "fire medicine." She now has three married sons and nine grandchildren. She has traveled much of the world, and she holds the distinction of being the first Aboriginal filmmaker in Australia.

"Along the many paths I have been drawn to over the course of my life have been politics, community development, health, housing, and education. However, it was in the arts that I excelled and found the most enjoyment. From writing I advanced into filmmaking," she relates.

Lorraine began her film career in 1973, when Aunt Millie asked her to make a film about some of the sacred sites of Australia that are being threatened by mining and development. "I wanted to fulfill Aunt Millie's request," Lorraine says, "and it all just came together, neat as you please."

Over the years, Lorraine has worked as an advisor and assistant for many critically acclaimed Australian films: *Journey among Women, The Last Wave, Chant of Jimmy Blacksmith, Women of the Sun*, and *Cyclone Tracey*. She has won awards for producing and directing two films: *Sacred Ground* and *Eelemarni*.

A central focus of Lorraine's current work is using her skills as a storyteller and a filmmaker to call attention to the plight of the Earth's protective energy grid through a film called *The Sickness Country*. The film will tell of the imminent threat posed by the mining of minerals from Coronation Hill, the head of the Rainbow Serpent.

Time to Tell Everyone

"We, the Australian Aboriginals, have been on our traditional land, the Land of the Everlasting Spirit, for tens of thousands of years," Lorraine explains. "Our culture is rivaled by no other, though we have been in seclusion for the last two hundred years. We are emerging from that seclusion now to show ourselves as no one has ever seen us. Our creation stories take us back into the Dreamtime, beginning when the Earth was one land mass. [Scientists place this phase of the Earth's development 250 to 300 million years ago, and they refer to the single land mass as Pangaea.] At that time, the four races—red, yellow, black, and white—lived side by side. There we lived as one people, creating a world of harmony, balance, and mystery.

"As Aboriginals, we have kept our culture intact for thousands of years, into the present time. Now we are becoming ready to share our wondrous culture with the other people of the world. That is my work through my teaching and my films.

"What a lot of people tend to forget is that my country has only been occupied for two hundred years by the British. It only took white people fifty years to destroy a million years of our culture, but the core of it still remains strong. We haven't forgotten. Our elders are telling us to go out and tell everyone so that no one can say they didn't hear."

Land of the Everlasting Spirit

Lorraine continues, "Whenever our elders, or shaman people—all our elders are shaman people—talk about our history and our beginning, our creation, they always talk about the time when the Earth was one land mass. They speak of the time before the cataclysm came that split the Earth up into the continents.

"This is our story, our mythology. Our land, Australia, is called Arunta, the Land of the Everlasting Spirit. Our old people tell us that we originally came from a planet that had seen its time and just blew up.

"See, our people were like refugees, and they went and lived in the stars in the Milky Way. Then seven spirit brothers and seven spirit sisters came to Earth. They came when the Earth was one big land mass.

"They came to erect an energy grid. Because, you see, the planet Earth is among the smallest of planets. And it is really not in the galactic system where all the other planets exist. We believe Earth is just a little bit outside the plane of the Milky Way galaxy in space. Because the Earth is so small, when the planets line up in a certain way the pull of galactic energy is so strong that it could just suck planet Earth into the spiral plane of the galactic system and toss it all around.

"So, my people were given the knowledge to create this energy grid because the planet that they were previously on did not have such a protective structure and it was destroyed. They realized that their new home, the Earth, needed to have such an energy grid in strong and healthy condition to withstand the periodic energy pulsations from the galaxy. Otherwise, it would quickly be drawn into the plane of the galaxy and experience devastating turbulence.

"But my ancestors had learned this lesson, and so they came to Earth to erect an energy grid, or an Earth truss, to help the Earth when it undergoes its changes. My ancestors' responsibility, and my people's responsibility still, is to the energy grid."

The Sacred Rainbow Serpent

The protective system that Lorraine refers to as an energy grid is a system of energy lines in and around the entire planet. As a system, it is similar to the meridians of energy in the human body that are used by practitioners of acupuncture. "In our old way," Lorraine says, "we call the energy grid Boamie, the sacred Rainbow Serpent, whose colors reflect the beauty of the Earth and sky, the rainbow.

The multicolored coils of the Rainbow Serpent are reflected in the precious stones that are concealed in the Earth's crust.

"It's called the Rainbow Serpent because it's got all the colors of the rainbow: the gold and silver, of course, and the diamonds, the rubies, the emeralds, and the uranium. You see, it's the foundation, the Earth's crust. They are the particular substances that keep the energy grid strong and the Earth solid when the planets line up every so often and threaten to draw the Earth into the galactic energy swirl.

"Since my people erected the energy grid, the Earth just sort of sails through the periodic planetary lineups without any difficulties. So that's my people's responsibility. Both men and women are very knowledgeable in how the energy grid works, the whole system. We know what each mineral in the Earth is supposed to do, and what men's and women's responsibilities are to keep the grid strong and healthy."

The Balance Is in Jeopardy

"We are very concerned about the energy grids of the Earth," Lorraine says. "They are there to help the Earth maintain balance. Crystals and other minerals feed energy to the energy grid. They have been used for millions of years that way. For the health of the Earth, the crystals must be free to let energy flow to the grid.

"But now minerals, metals, and jewels have been removed from the Earth to such an extent that the balance is in jeopardy. Uranium, in particular, is important for this task. When it is all gone, the Earth will be right out of balance."

Since the advent of nuclear power in the 1930s and 1940s, extensive mining projects have burrowed into sources of uranium in many sensitive sites around the world. These areas include the ancestral land of the Hopi Indians in the U.S. Southwest, the high Himalayas long guarded by the Tibetan lamas, and the sacred lands of the Australian Aborigines. For example, Kakadu National Park in the Northern Territories is one of Australia's famed beauty spots, and it attracts thousands of visitors every year. It also forms part of the traditional land of the Jawoyn people, who, like all Aboriginal peoples, trace their ancestry back some forty thousand years. These days, the Jawoyn refer sorrowfully to their land as "the sickness country"—hence the name of Lorraine's film.

On paper, at least, Kakadu is territory belonging to the British crown, which can lease it out to Australian and foreign interests. There is intense interest in the area, for it is rich in platinum, palladium, and uranium.

Lorraine says all of these coveted substances are critical components of the Rainbow Serpent, the protective energy grid. In fact, according to the Aborigines, this site is the most sacred and critical in Australia. The British coincidentally named it Coronation Hill, but for many thousands of years the Aborigines have known it as the crown, or head, of Boamie, the Rainbow Serpent.

According to the elders of the Jawoyn people, Coronation Hill is part of an extremely powerful dreaming that, if disturbed, will cause sickness, fires, earthquakes, and volcanic eruptions that will obliterate wide areas of the Earth.

For years, the Jawoyn people have been struggling to keep mining interests away from Coronation Hill. Two uranium mines have already been opened, and the decade of the 1990s is bringing more threats.

The Jawoyn people had hoped that by compromising with tourism, for which they receive no monetary gain, they could soften any governmental hard-line attitude on mining. But the requirements of the modern material world are in sharp conflict with the spiritual vision of these Earth-based peoples. The issue at stake, as ever, is the concept of land ownership.

Even beyond land ownership and the long-lived and deadly poisonous effects of nuclear waste, Lorraine believes there are other critical considerations in this matter: "This mining has an influence on the human race, too, and the human body. The human being is a link between the heavens and the Earth. By keeping our bodies in balance and harmony, we can keep the Earth healthy, and that in turn supports our health. You see, it's a cycle. I use crystals in healing, but I do not believe they should be taken from the Earth to be used as ornaments. It's more valuable to leave them in the Earth. The same with the uranium."

At a Crucial Juncture

Based on her traditional training and her meetings with Aboriginal elders, Lorraine says we are again at a crucial juncture in the Earth's development. "We have been told that within every one million years, there is a seven-thousand-year-long Earth shift. Then we begin to go into a new world, like we are doing now. By our reckoning, we are actually at the end of a seven-thousand-year shift now, and we are beginning to enter a new million-year-long epoch.

"Our people and our teachings are very similar to the teachings of the North American Indian people. But we have different interpretations, and we know our responsibility: taking care of the Earth through the energy grids. It's very similar to what the Native Americans teach about. We do that by giving thanks to the Earth through songs, dances, and ceremonies.

"Right now there's two things. The Earth is undergoing its Earth changes, which is normal for this time in our development. But because there's been so much destruction to the energy grid, especially the gold, which is nearly exhausted already—and now they are after the uranium—there is great danger to the stability of the Earth.

"Gold has driven men mad for thousands of years, leading them to lie, steal, cheat, murder, and make war… all this wickedness to get the gold. Humanity has become greedy and, as a result, wicked. That has led to fighting, war, and disease. People have forgotten their responsibility to the Earth for want of the gold. And now it's the uranium.

"As a consequence of all this mining, there's not enough of the Rainbow Serpent left to help the Earth undergo its seven-thousand-year shift in a safe way. It's all topsy-turvy. Without the balance of the minerals and a healthy energy grid, we cannot pass through the current planetary alignments, and we may be drawn into the plane of the galaxy.

"As well as the Earth, humanity has to go through its changes. We've all got to rejuvenate and to create a new world on this same physical substance. And we are going through it. There's no safe place on Earth. We've just got to ride it out. But if we are in balance within ourselves, and in balance with the Earth, then we are healthy.

"At the end of each change—every time we come into a new world—the Great Creator says, 'OK, humanity, you must start your change now, too, and go into the new world. But you must do it in accordance with the Earth, as well as yourself, with heart.'"

The Story of Wollombin

With a steely look of certainty, Lorraine says that one of the secrets that needs to be revealed now is the story of Wollombin, or Mount Warning, and the spirit of Waugatha, who is said to inhabit this sacred mountain.

"If you go back to the time when the Earth split up from one land mass into the continents, it was another time of Earth changes. Humanity was wicked in those days, too. Even your own books in Western civilization speak of Noah and the ark and how there was wickedness on the Earth.

"The Native American people say they rode the changes out on the back of a turtle—a land mass like a turtle, Turtle Island. My people rode the flood out by climbing upon a big red rock called Uluru—now usually called Ayer's Rock. Uluru simply means 'the big rock.' Uluru is seven miles around and one mile up.

"Our people teach that when the Earth was one big land mass, Wollombin was one of four big mountains that housed huge crystals. They are the activators for the crystal grid and for the energy grid that protects the Earth. Perhaps the Himalayas might have one, and perhaps the Andes in South America might have one. I don't know for sure, but I know Wollombin is one, the one in the East. We are east of the rest of the world in our tradition, but I don't know what the other mountains are.

"When the Earth split, people were running in confusion, and some of my people stayed on other continents—though they are all extinct now. And some other nationalities stayed Down Under, but now they are extinct, too. But as our old people recall, when the people ran, a White Buffalo ran with them in Australia."

As recorded voluminously in the lore of the Lakota, the Crow, the Chippewa, and many other Native American tribes, the White

Buffalo is one of their most sacred symbols. It represents purity, as well as sacrifice for the benefit of all the people. The White Buffalo is regarded as a sign that prayers are being heard and that the promises of prophecy are being fulfilled.

According to Aboriginal legend, at the time the Earth broke up and the White Buffalo ran with the people, a sacred mountain that was under the care of the North American Indian people also broke off and came with them. Instead of remaining with the North American continent of the Red Race, it stayed on the east coast of what is known today as Australia, the Land of the Everlasting Spirit.

"That mountain is Wollombin, or Mount Warning," Lorraine says. "And it is the mountain of which Aunt Millie Boyd is custodian. See, the story of that mountain has been handed down for thousands of years, through the generations. At the time that mountain split off with the Australian continent, there was a very high, powerful shaman or medicine man of the Indian people who stayed on that mountain. Wollombin, you see, means "eagle." The spirit is still there, and his name is Waugatha.

"That mountain is in my aunt's country. She's the last custodian of it, though, now that it has been handed back into the care of the North American Indian people. You see, I came here to America in 1988 to look and see if there was any memory among the Indian people of their lost mountain. And there was someone here, a medicine man, who remembered. I found him. Ever since, there have been Indian people who have come to visit the mountain and who have met with Aunt Millie to hear about and learn about Wollombin and Waugatha. See, there's the connection between Australia and North America—between the Aborigines and the Native Americans. It has something to do with the Native American relationship to the sun and the Sun Dance."

Aboriginal Persecution

Lorraine continued her story. "Prior to 1975, we were governed by the government. A group of white people set themselves up as the governing body over the Aboriginals in 1816, and they called themselves the Aboriginal Protection Board. Now, they started out with very good intentions, because at that time there were a lot of massacres going on with my people. We were practically wiped out. So this governing agency formed themselves into a board, and to protect us they placed us on missions, which are much the same thing as the Indian reservations in America.

"Where missions and reservations are concerned, it's exactly the same with the North American Indian people and my people, the Aboriginal people. The Aboriginal Protection Board was finally abolished in 1967. But prior to that the board had become very oppressive. The rules were that Aboriginals could not own land, could not own money or receive money, and could not be educated. Aboriginal children were removed from their parents, placed in institutions, and trained as domestics and laborers—a slave class, based on the Negro race system in America. You see, the British came here to America, but they sent their convicts to my country. We got the worst of the worst."

Aborigines in Australia have suffered under terrible persecution since England established its penal colonies there two hundred years ago. Over the years, the Aborigines have been attacked, herded onto reserves much like the American Indian reservations, and discriminated and legislated against. In many instances they have been forced into slavery. They are still engaged in an ongoing struggle for land rights—rights they say are essential for the well-being of the world.

"We were freed in 1967 after a referendum," Lorraine says. "We were freed from the missions. We can go anywhere now, but before that we needed permission—a twenty-four-hour citizen's pass to go anywhere, to move. Even though life was terrible on the missions, they allowed our people to keep the language, the traditions, the culture, the law, everything going—despite all the pressures.

"We adopted some of the Christianity that was pressed upon us. We went to church and Sunday school. We listened to the doctrine, but we never accepted it, because we only have one God, one Creator, and nobody in between. I could be corrected here, but, as I understand it, Australian Aboriginal people and Native American Indian people did not follow Christian teachings by and large, nor did they follow a leader like Jesus, Buddha, or Mohammed. We never did worship a human being. We stuck to one God in heaven and one Mother Earth. And we carried out our responsibility to the animals, the birds, the fish, and to Mother Earth. As far as I know."

A Council of Elders

"Our elders met in 1975 in the capital city, Canberra, and drew together over 350 of the Aboriginal people," Lorraine recounts. "At that time they gave out their predictions of the changes that are happening and coming. It was a closed meeting just with us Aboriginal people. What they said is exactly what the Native American people are saying. When the Earth undergoes its last Earth shift—very soon—some of the land mass will go under, just as in ancient times Atlantis went under the water. At the same time, other land masses will rise, which will bring the continents back closer. Australia will be east, then, of America.

"Back in 1975, the elders, seven of them, sat in a circle in the center. The spokesman stood up and looked at us and said, 'Which way are we going to go in the future?' And then he threw into the center of the circle first a Bible and then a little bark painting—which is the way our people have recorded things since ancient times.

"I thought, 'Gee, he's asking us to make a choice between religion and our culture.' But that wasn't it. Their philosophy was that the Bible and our teachings are the same as God's law. I didn't understand that for nearly fifteen years. But now I know. I realize and understand what the old people were saying.

"I resisted at first and thought, 'No way am I going to try and teach white people all this about Wollombin and Waugatha, the energy grid and all the rest. Wouldn't I be selling out, or be betraying my ancestral heritage?'

"But back in 1975, the elders said, 'You will know, when the time comes, what decision to make.' And whatever it was, it would be fine by them because each and every white person must know our story and our teachings before we go into the new world. Despite all that's happened to our people, our elders said that we must teach the white people our culture. We've got to all go into the new world as one people. We were told to go out and start teaching because, as our elders put it, 'Not one white person should turn around and say to us, "We were not told. We were not warned."'

"Our elders said, at that very same meeting, that once all humanity settles down into the Earth changes, then industry goes, commerce goes, money goes, governing bodies go. North American Indian people and Aboriginal people will be among the leaders in power, in politics, in government—but not the way it is now. They said we would go back to a cultural beginning, to meeting again in a circle, in the Sacred Hoop. It was all mind blowing to us then, in 1975, but it has made more and more sense as time has gone on."

The Predictions

As she meets with groups in America and around the world, Lorraine shares some of the predictions that were voiced at the Canberra meeting of the Aborigines: "As of 1975, our old people started to tell us of the changes that would come about in our country. They spoke of the great droughts that would come, and the breakdown in the energy grid. The elders spoke of all the trends of the Great Purification that the Hopi Indian people and others talk about.

"So far, many of the major things that they mentioned have come to pass. The greatest and most important thing they said was that our young men would shed their blood for our land, but not in a warlike way. We Aboriginal people have never been warlike. We have just continued to support the energy grid, and we have made a deliberate decision not to involve ourselves in hierarchies or power struggles or establishing an army. It was always peace, equality, companionship, and love—all based specifically on love, the great emotional binder. We stuck to God's laws, like the Ten Commandments. The First Commandment is universal: Thou shalt not kill. There's no exceptions. We've always obeyed that law.

"What's happening in Australia is that the Ku Klux Klan is very strong. They use that name 'Down Under,' too. The Klan has established itself very strongly in my country, and you know what their philosophy is: hate and all that sort of stuff. There are many groups and committees whose aim is to keep Australia white. Now, how they got that idea, when we were there so long before them, I will never understand.

"Anyway, they out and out began to go after us and the Vietnamese boat people. The Klan operates out of every prison in Australia. In recent years, there have been over 260 deaths of our young people—deaths in custody. That aspect is very damaging to our people. And now the Klan is showing themselves elsewhere, especially in the outback, in the little towns.

"That's all part of the prophecy of our old people. With the Ku Klux Klan, of course, comes the occult, black medicine, black magic, and all that sort of stuff. That also is part of the prophecy, because evil, too, has got to make itself or break itself before the year 2000.

"Part of the prophecy from our people is that it will be the children of the world who will suffer at the hands of evil before the year 2000. If you look at it from a world perspective, and take Chernobyl, you'll begin to see. Our old people predicted Chernobyl in 1975, and now it's the children of Chernobyl that are suffering. Thousands of them are coming down with leukemia in Russia and Europe. I don't care if the Russians or whoever say they're responsible; it's Australia that's ultimately responsible for Chernobyl because the uranium comes from there, from our land. It should never have been dug up.

"When our old people said the world would suffer, the children would suffer, they looked at it that way because they started from home. So, the children of the world are suffering. They are the seeds of the new world. Likewise, you've probably heard of the plight of the Romanian children, and in America there is so much child abuse. It's all over the world. That's what our old people were talking about in 1975."

Come to Wollombin

According to Lorraine, each Aboriginal tribe has a responsibility. In a tribe, one person looks after the environment, one caretakes the animals, one looks after the fish of the sea, and so on for all the other dimensions of life and creation. "The last person who was caretaker in my father's tribe, the Bundjalung, was my father's niece, whose name was Mary Wilson. We called her Sister Mary, and she passed away in 1991. She was the last custodian for the dolphins.

"Two years before Harmonic Convergence in 1987, Sister Mary was told by the dolphins that something very big was going to happen related to the Earth changes. They didn't tell her what it was. But my Aunt Millie was also told to prepare Wollombin for a big happening related to Earth changes.

"Aunt Millie told me in 1986 to look for a Thunder Rock, a Thunder Egg, and to place it in the East, at the base of Wollombin [Mount Warning]. So we did that. I found the rock, which was a geode about the size of a loaf of bread, and we placed it at the base of Wollombin in the East.

"I work in education sometimes, so I was invited to an education conference in New Zealand. It was at a big center, and I was looking at all the fliers tacked to the wall, and one caught my eye. The words seemed strange to me, and they still seem strange, for it talked about Harmonic Convergence and Quetzalcoatl, the Rainbow Feathered Serpent of the Americas. Then I got a message from Spirit that this was the big happening that we were told to prepare Wollombin for.

"I copied the flier and took it back to Aunt Millie and spread the word to come to Wollombin at Harmonic Convergence. Among the New Age people in Australia, the message went out that Uluru was the focal point, and that's where everyone should gather. But we knew that Wollombin was the place. All these esoteric people jumped on the bandwagon and sent everyone to Uluru. But we just said no."

Waiting Through the Night

"We got it all organized," Lorraine says. "We encouraged as many people as possible to go to Wollombin for Harmonic Convergence. That was part of what the old people were talking about in 1975. We got over six hundred people there, and we stayed opposite the mountain. We didn't stay where all the people were camping. There were too many people; we wouldn't have been able to breathe, let alone talk. So a group of us Aboriginal people sat all night on the other side of the mountain the night before Harmonic Convergence.

We were told something was going to happen on the mountain, so we waited.

"About quarter past two or half past two in the morning, we noticed that it was getting bright. You see, the mountain looks over the ocean, and we were slightly inland. As it started to get bright, I looked at Aunt Millie, because it was not time for the moon to rise. There was only half a moon then—not much, but it was pretty bright. As we watched, we saw, at first, a fire like the sun rising. It was as bright as if the sun was coming up.

"What happened in a split second was that the moon and the sun moved. The moon started to set and the sun started to rise, even at this early hour. They came—bang!—together, then dropped. We thought that was something, that's OK, it came to pass. Then we saw a silver beam coming out of the mountain, and the silver beam changed into Waugatha, the Native American spirit who resides on the mountain. Then it gradually slithered into the snake, and Waugatha changed to the human, and then, all of a sudden, Wollombin and the eagle as one. It all came together as one on the top—the silver beam, the Rainbow Feathered Serpent, or Quetzalcoatl, and Waugatha.

"For us, this was a confirmation that the mountain belongs to the Red Race. Aunt Millie then said it was time to tell everyone the story of Wollombin and Waugatha and who really owns that mountain. That's also when Aunt Millie decided that the care of the mountain should be handed back to the Red Race.

"When I started being trained as a healer, one of my teachers said I would travel the world to share and teach and learn. Auntie Millie said to be sure and tell the North American people about this mountain, and that the responsibility for caring for it was no longer ours. This I have done, everywhere I have traveled. I've met many Indian people, and I've told them."

The New World Has Started

Lorraine says Harmonic Convergence signaled the end of the old world. "The Earth is starting its repairs. It needed human help on August 16 and 17, 1987, because the only mineral that hasn't been taken too much is, thank goodness, the crystal.

"Elders from all points on the Earth began to meet at sacred sites on their own land in 1988 to make prayers and ceremonies. The ancient people are seeing that now they have to come together and make world decisions. We have to go back to our Dreamtime culture before we can come forward. All the tribal elders from around the world are beginning to come together and to meet as one big committee of elders to determine the cultural beginning of the new world, the New Age.

"The new world has started. Teaching, politics, and education are eventually going to be based on the laws and politics of this international committee of elders."

According to Lorraine, the people of the world can help the transition to the new time by helping to prevent the mining of the Rainbow Serpent—helping to ensure that there will be no more unconscious mining of uranium and other precious materials. The Australian government has promised the Aborigines that it will not mine. But whenever there is an economic slump, they think the only way out of that slump is to exploit the Earth—to mine the uranium at sites like Coronation Hill, the crown of the Rainbow Serpent. "That's the pressure that's being put on our people," Lorraine says, "and on all the people of Australia.

"When we say we want land rights, what we really want is the right to protect that land—not so much for our own gain, because materialism is not part of our culture. We didn't care when we weren't allowed money. Money was insignificant to us. If we got it, poof, it was gone: we spread it around among all the people. We tried to go into these national parks and explain about the sacred sites and the energy grid, and to say that because of this they were dangerous sites to dig into the Earth. But they don't listen.

"Harmonic Convergence brought the world's attention to the necessity of energizing the Earth's energy grid and of reconstructing the intricate systems protecting the balance of the Earth—Grandmother Spider's web system, to use the Native American way of speaking about this."

As Lorraine sees it, there are other ways modern people can help restore the health of the web, or energy grid, so that we may pass through this time of transition in better order. "First," she says, "go to the elders. Listen to what the elders say. Here in America and around the world, listen to the elders. And then make prayers and ceremonies for the Earth. Take action. Plant trees and flowers. Good diet, proper exercise, and prayer can also help us to stabilize our lives so that we may offer them in service toward stabilizing life on Earth."

What She Was Shown

In 1984, Lorraine was gifted with a powerful vision. "What I was shown," she says, "was a vision similar to visions I have heard many Native Americans speak about. I was shown this outer circle representing the women and the next circle in representing the men. Then there's a little circle in the center, which is the children. Now, this is symbolic of what the new world is going to look like. It's going to be a beautiful golden world.

"Most people will be in the four golden rays of this circle. But those who are still trying to sort themselves out and find the meaning of their lives will be in between the golden rays, waiting. These areas are all in motion. The rays in between the golden rays are purple rays or violet rays. The people who are in the violet rays have the opportunity to push through and step into the golden rays when they make their minds up. That's because this golden world has to be pure. So this lot in the violet rays are given the opportunity to choose. This whole violet ray has got to be cleared by the year 1999. That's what we believe. It'll happen that fast. The elders feel that we will pass through this time of transition OK, even if they mine uranium at Coronation Hill, the head of the Rainbow Serpent.

"This is part of the purification. In the back of the Bible, the book of Revelation talks about the Heavenly Host. Now, the Heavenly Host, as our elders explain them to us, are our planetary helpers who get their direction from the Creator, God. God told our planetary helpers, the Heavenly Host, only to monitor and support the Earth. They do not interfere with humanity. We have spirit helpers, too. They are our ancestors' spirits or the spirits of anybody who is not living in a body now. Spirit helpers are the ones who look after humanity. You see, our Heavenly Host does not interfere with the spiritual development and destiny of humanity. They only monitor the Earth and Earth movements.

"The Native Americans refer to the Great Mystery, but our people always refer to God as the Beloved One. The Beloved One said to the Heavenly Host, 'I will not let my Earth be destroyed.' So God asked the Heavenly Host only to monitor the Earth and see that it gets safely through.

"So there may be volcanoes and earthquakes and storms and diseases and the hate groups, but we get through it all because the Spir-

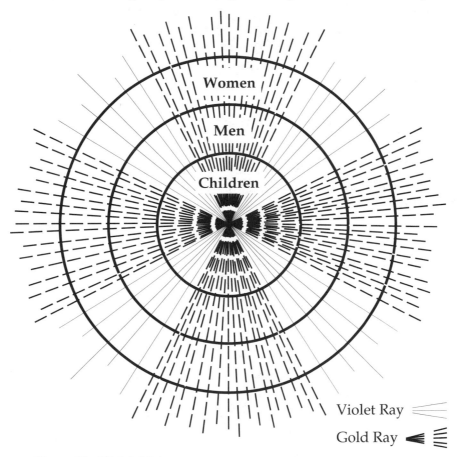

Figure 10. Alinta's Vision.

it will illuminate the wars, the Ku Klux Klan, the diseases, and all that. Some will perish; they'll go altogether; they'll die. But some will live. There's a real demand that we wake up and listen closely and follow our hearts and spirits.

"Right now there are four areas of gold and four areas of the violet ray. But that will all close in a circle when it's ready. That will all become one pure golden world, one circle, the Sacred Hoop.

"Each indigenous race will have its own system, its own interpretations or teachings, its own way. The Earth will be guided by a council of eight elders, one woman and one man from each of the four races. That's the Aboriginal way of seeing things."

"In the new world, the form of communication will be with computers, TVs, and so forth. People will use the technology that is the gift of the light-skinned race to communicate with each other and with Spirit. The gifts of all the races will be honored and used, too. This is the rainbow of humanity. This is what our old people say."

As It Was in the Beginning

Despite all the upheaval of the Earth changes, Lorraine is filled with hope. She says that watching the rainbows, and supporting them with prayer and stewardship of the Earth, are two things that anyone can do in these troubled times. "The rainbow is a form of illumination for humanity. One of the signs our elders looked for in ancient times was a perfect rainbow, a perfect one. They do ceremonies periodically to keep the energy grid healthy. They would use the rainbows to monitor what they had done. If they did the ceremonies right and the energy grid was healthy, then the rainbows would be perfect. Some of our old people could summon up the rainbow the way some Native American medicine people could bring rain. My father was one that could bring rain. Others could bring the rainbow with their prayers.

"As soon as the rainbow appeared, our elders would look at it closely, carefully, for little flaws. Were all the colors as bright as they should be? Did the rainbow arc from one place on the Earth to another, or was it incomplete? They'd size it up carefully. That way they could see if Boamie, the Rainbow Serpent, needed something—

if it was damaged or incomplete in some way. They could tell that by studying the rainbow in the sky for imperfections. The rainbow in the sky is a reflection of the Rainbow Serpent of the Earth; it reflects the health of the Earth and its energy grid."

Lorraine says this may be the reason that, when we see rainbows in the modern world, they are so often dull or distorted. Or, they do not reach completely from one point on the Earth to another point; only one end of the rainbow touches the ground. The rainbow is a reflection of the health of the Earth underneath it, and in many places the Earth is sick now.

"Whenever our old people were traveling, or were out and about," Lorraine says, "they'd call up the rainbow and check the energy grid. That was their responsibility. It was an ongoing thing, and it's ongoing today.

"The rainbows will be perfect again as soon as the Sacred Hoop closes, as soon as the golden circle of the new world is complete. It will be perfect. The Earth will already have undergone its changes and all that sort of thing. It will be rejuvenating, giving new life. The rainbow will again encircle the Earth perfectly, as it was in the beginning."

NINE

Blossoms Unfold
in An Age of Flowers

While the notion that we live in a prophesied time of transition is widely accepted among native elders, the terminology they use to describe the transition varies widely. Like Seneca Grandmother Twylah Nitsch, many believe we are moving from the Fourth World to the Fifth World. Other native wisdom keepers say we are moving into the world of the Sixth Sun. The Maya call this time the New Itza Age, Christians call it the Tribulation, astrologers call it the Age of Aquarius, Buddhists call it Shambhala, and booksellers call it the New Age. Yet another name for this time arises from Native American culture; it's a name that may ultimately unite the various mythologies: the Age of Flowers.

In a book entitled *Beneath the Sun and Under the Moon*, author Tony Shearer says the sacred calendar of the Native Americans offers us no hint about the character of the next epoch. If, however, we consider the theme suggested by the name Age of Flowers, a number of clues about the unfolding world epoch do emerge.

Cherokee teacher Dhyani Ywahoo of Vermont has spent much time contemplating the calendars and the start of the new cycle. "For us," she says, "Harmonic Convergence was the ending of one fire and the start of a new fire—part of an ongoing cycle of change. According to the Native American calendar, we have entered a new cycle of Thirteen Heavens, a New Age in which we have the opportunity to let go of aggression and fear and begin to live a life of enlightened consciousness. The cycle that began in 1987 created an opening in the mind's eye so we can see more clearly our unity. Lots of traditions were sharing. Many people came together and saw the common threads that bind us. The next step is to actually do it—to take the inner vision and make it real in the outer world through right action."

Dhyani is not only a respected teacher in the Etowah Cherokee tradition but also an acknowledged master of Tibetan Buddhism. She says that many Native Americans have paid close attention to the transition described in the Native American calendar. "The age ending has been a time when people have gathered information about building and about inventions to make

Photo 16. Dhyani Ywahoo. *Photo by Pamela Cabel-Whiting © 1986.*

life better. Now it's a time for people to recognize that the inventions are a creation of mind, to put aside such inventions as cause harm, and to bring forth and further develop those activities that benefit all beings and benefit the future generations."

"We are moving around the spiral, coming again to a place of whole civilization, of true planetary consciousness. What we see now are the fever throes, the end of the fever's nightmares as the sickness and poisons leave the system. And just how well the culture, the people go through this time is really dependent upon the calling of the light, because in a time of purification the light makes clear the places of darkness.

"How much the planet will suffer, how much the people will suffer, is really determined by the consciouness of groups. It is no longer a matter of just individuals finding the light within themselves; it's really necessary to establish a network, to rebuild those areas of the Earth's web that have been harmed by unclear thinking.

"According to the way we are taught, and the seeds that are being planted, the new calendar that has begun is to manifest peace—an age of peace. The elders have asked—this is a large council of elders, so they speak to Central and North American people—that the morning after every full moon, at about 10 a.m., we gather flowers and go outside and look to the sun, to the flowers, and to the heart of the Earth. In so doing, we bring more solar energy and flower wisdom to the Earth, because the New Age is the Age of Flowers.

"Flowers give light and joy. They also have a very subtle consciousness. They have a unity of mind. Flower energy is peaceful, and flowers are great medicine. By meditation on flowers, we can reduce the inflammation caused by aggressive habits of mind. Flowers are our medicine for the next age. In this new time, flowers will become very significant as teachers and healers of humanity.

"Flowers move with the sun; thus, they have a certain committed solar consciousness. They know the proper relationship between Spirit and Earth. The flowers remind us to look up to heaven and to actualize the solar energy in our own lives—to speak more clearly and to act more clearly.

"Flowers are the medicine we need for balance and tone. The old people say that when properly prepared—and some of the preparations can take as long as twelve years—flower essences can widen the frequency response of the human mind. They increase our sensitivity. But they need to be prepared with prayer, right offering, and dedication. Flowers can remove the poisons of incorrect thought and stir the body to its fullest health."

The Quickening

"Basically, these are still times for planting seeds of good relationship," Dhyani says. "Those who are responding to the teachings of the flowers are establishing a parallel government of people who are committed to peace and generating that energy."

According to Dhyani, one way the flowers are teaching humanity is through their pollen. In recent years, as the ozone has thinned and caused weakening of the human immune system, doctors have reported a sharp increase in the number of cases of hay fever and other allergies. As Dhyani explains, "Through the movement of flower pollen in the air, we are all being quickened. That quickening for some is frightening, and it also brings a reaction—just like when someone takes a homeopathic remedy. First, they may become a little bit sicker—but it's really the sickness being exaggerated so that the organism can be awakened to heal itself.

"The whole issue of allergy," she says, "is really an issue of the planetary system and not the human system. In some instances the Earth and the people are so out of alignment with one another that anything natural is disturbing to the human body. For years we've been taking artificial vitamins, and for years the food has been grown with artificial fertilizers. So the natural kingdom has been made an enemy, and the body and the immune system respond as if nature were an enemy. This is a result of years and years of improper drugging of the crops.

"I also think that's why there's so much of an increase in addictions among people. Because the plants are jazzed up, people get into the habit of being jazzed up. Then they start looking for more and more stimulants or depressants to continue that cycle. People who are in their forties today are the people who were eating in their formative years the most highly sprayed and the most highly chemically treated food that this world has ever seen. There's only so much that the human body can take.

"By releasing their pollen, flowers are trying to attract the attention of human beings. The plants do that specifically. Plants do have minds, and they have alertness and consciousness," Dhyani says, "and they can change. Notice also that the atmosphere's quality is changing. Certainly there's less oxygen. There are more heavy metals and acid in the air. So the plants are working even harder to transmute these things, and in their efforts for transformation the plants that survive become more potent."

Dhyani and others have suggested that at some point a particular flower or flowers may be developed as healing potions—not so much for individuals, but rather for distressed areas of the planet. The preparations may be made and used as offerings to abused locations on the planet, such as old toxic waste sites, to help restore ecological balance.

If these planetary remedies are developed at some point during the Age of Flowers, Dhyani believes that the inner attitude of the people who offer the flowers will be critical. "It's not just the substance of the flower or the crystal or the water or anything," she explains, "it's also the intention with which these things are applied. It all needs the direction of clarified mind so that it can bring the result that is beneficial. That's why the elders always reminded us that prayer is important."

Jitterbug Perfume

In the late 1980s, bestselling author Tom Robbins published a novel entitled *Jitterbug Perfume*. The book contains a chapter with a peculiar title: *"Dannyboy's Theory (Where We Are Going and Why It Smells the Way It Does)."* In that chapter, the author contends that humankind is about to enter the floral stage of its evolutionary development.

Although the book is a novel, Robbins offers some plain facts about human brains and the quality of their consciousness. Specifically, through his characters, he notes that reptile consciousness is cold, aggressive, self-preserving, angry, greedy, and paranoid. Neurophysicist Paul McLean has pointed out that within their skulls human beings still harbor a fully intact and functional reptilian brain: the limbic lobe, the hypothalamus, and perhaps other organs of the diencephalon. When we are in a cold sweat or a blind rage, he says, our reptile brain is in control of our consciousness.

Robbins writes that human beings also have a mammal brain, called the midbrain or mesencephalon, and that characteristics of mammal consciousness are warmth, generosity, loyalty, love, joy, grief, humor, pride, competition, and appreciation of art and music. In late mammalian times—the last several thousand years—human beings developed a third brain, the telencephalon, consisting principally of the neocortex, a dense rind of nerve fibers about an eighth of an inch thick. This part of the brain is molded over the top of the existing mammal brain.

Brain researchers are greatly puzzled by the neocortex. What is its function? And why has it developed? In his book, Robbins concludes that the third brain is a floral brain, corresponding to the evolving stage of human development.

Flowers extract energy from light. Likewise, neuromelanin—one of the principal chemicals in this part of the brain—absorbs light and also has the capacity to convert light into other forms of energy. Consequently, Robbins notes, the neocortex is light sensitive and can itself be lit up by higher forms of mental activity such as meditation or chanting. Thus, he writes, "the ancients were not being metaphoric when they referred to 'illumination.'"

In *Jitterbug Perfume*, Robbins asserts that we are moving gradually toward a dominant floral consciousness: "We require a less physically aggressive, less rugged human being now. We need a more relaxed, contemplative, gentle, flexible kind of person, for only he or she can survive (and expedite) this very new system that is upon us. Only he or she can participate in the next evolutionary phase. It has definite spiritual overtones, this floral phase of consciousness. . . .

"Flowers do not see, hear, taste, or touch, but they react to light in a crucial manner, and they direct their lives and their environment through an orchestration of aroma. . . . We live now in an information technology. Flowers have *always* lived in an information technology. Flowers gather information all day. At night, they process it. This is called photosynthesis.

"As our neocortex comes into full use, we, too, will practice a kind of photosynthesis. As a matter of fact, we already do, but compared to the flowers, our kind is primitive and limited. For one thing, information gathered from daily newspapers, soap operas, sales conferences, and coffee klatsches is inferior to information gathered from sunlight. (Since all matter is condensed light, light is the source, the cause of life. Therefore, light is divine. The flowers have a direct line to God that an evangelist would kill for.)

"With reptile consciousness," Robbins concludes, "we had hostile confrontation. With mammal consciouness, we had civilized debate. With floral consciousness, we'll have empathetic telepathy."

A Modality of Healing

Since the early part of the twentieth century, flowers have in fact emerged as an effective modality of healing. Specifically, in the late 1920s a British doctor began experimenting with flowers as remedies for human disease. The results of his experiments opened a whole new field of health care that began to blossom just as the 1980s were ending.

Edward Bach, M.D. (1886-1936), practiced traditional medicine from 1914 until 1918, when he became interested in homeopathy, the healing modality founded on the principle that like cures like: in other words, that small doses of whatever is causing a problem, intelligently applied, can bring about a positive healing reaction within the body.

Bach was an outstanding doctor, held in high regard by both orthodox and homeopathic physicians. In 1928, he became interested in flowers and began to prepare homeopathic remedies from various blossoms. As time went on, he observed excellent results from these medicines. Working steadily until the time of his death in 1936, he developed thirty-eight individual flower essences as well as the popular Rescue Remedy, a combination of several flowers used to alleviate trauma.

Bach believed that bodily ills were only symptoms. He wrote that the ills of the heart and the spirit should instead be the focus of a healer's attention: "It is our fears, our cares, our anxieties, and such like that open the path to the invasion of illness." Dr. Bach also believed that the overweening materialism of our times has caused us to focus almost exclusively on the physical aspects of disease and to pay scant attention to the underlying or spiritual causes.

In response to this perception, Bach developed a new branch of herbal and homeopathic medicine that employed flowers to relieve mental distress. With this system, problems could be dealt with on an inner level. Specifically, he created his flower remedies to heal attitudes such as anger, resentment, remorse, lack of confidence, greed, and anxiety. Bach believed that by correcting harmful mental attitudes, one could prevent a disease from becoming established in the body. If one treated a disease at the energy level, he posited, one could avoid having to deal with it later as a gross physical malady.

How the Flowers May Heal Us

Flower essences are part of an evolving branch of the healing arts known as vibrational medicine. With vibrational healing, the subtle energies of the human body are influenced, gently and unobtrusively, through such means as color, light, sound, and flowers. These healing modalities are based on the understanding that our state of health is a reflection of our alignment with the universal laws of truth and the degree to which we are fulfilling our soul's destiny in a balanced way. The more precise our alignment, according to floral healing theory, the more easily our soul energies can radiate through us as good health or wholeness. In this understanding, illnesses or diseases are seen as outward manifestations of the different levels of tension that have accumulated within us. They reflect where we are out of alignment with the truth of our lives and the world.

One leading organization in the development of flowers as a healing modality is the Alaskan Flower Essence Project. The project describes their understanding in vivid terms: "Flowers," they write, "are light patterns of truth, beautifully expressed in physical form."

Flowers are the highest, most beautiful, most refined part of plants. They are said to correspond to the human soul. Flower essences influence the electrical energy field of the human body in much the same way acupuncture does, albeit more gently and less obtrusively.

Flower essences are easy to prepare. All that is required is pure water, a glass bowl, sunlight, and fresh blossoms. The blossoms are harvested in a respectful way and then floated upon the water in the bowl and placed in the sunlight. The healing light of the sun helps transmit the particular energetic essence of the flowers into the water, potentizing it so it can be used for healing. The resulting flower essences are liquid plant preparations that convey the distinct imprint of the particular flower from which they are made. They expand a person's capacity to interweave the spiritual, mental, emotional, and physical aspects of wellness.

Dr. Bach developed remedies employing flowers such as Wild Rose, Clematis, Heather, Cherry Plum, Gorse, and Honeysuckle. In recent years, groups such as the Alaskan Flower Essence Project, the Flower Essence Society, Pegasus, and Perelandra have taken the art and science of healing with flowers much further. Their approach to healing through the personality of the patient has proven itself over and over, demonstrating the efficacy of flower essences in thousands of cases.

Flowers become an evolutionary force in the consciousness of the person who uses them. They are not the cause of the healing or the health that results from their use; rather, they are agents that support the free will and clear intention of the person who seeks to heal him or herself.

The Soul of Nature

Richard Katz and Patricia Kaminski are the founders of the Flower Essence Society (FES). Through this organizational vehicle, they support research and educational programs that deepen our understanding of flowers as a medium for healing.

FES teaches that flower essences address health in a broad sense by strengthening the link between body and soul. The organization professes that flowers can be used to treat a wide variety of disorders such as stress, addictions, depression, fear, emotional repression, and jealousy. They can also be used to enhance creativity and spiritual awareness.

"With flower essences," Richard Katz comments, "we are seeking to bring spiritual light into our lives. Forty years ago, with the nuclear explosion, we split apart matter to create light. Now the generation that was born in that time has matured and is deciding whether to continue to split apart matter to create light or to radiate it from within. Never has the choice been clearer."

If this is the Age of Flowers, and if flowers are to become our healers and teachers, then what have we got to learn? As Richard Katz sees it, "Flowers are the soul of nature, and they give it expression through color, form, and fragrance. Flower essences are the art and science of bringing the balance of nature to the human soul.

"Most remedies are intended to make us feel better, but flower essences can help us heal our souls and find our life direction.

Perhaps the most healing experience you can have is to be aware of your life purpose."

To help a person develop awareness of and take steps toward fulfilling his or her life purpose, Katz recommends one of three specific flower essences, or a combination of all three: mullein, walnut, and wild oat. He suggests that the person place a few drops of the flower essences under the tongue and then relax, repeating this process rhythmically, several times a day for several weeks, to internalize the subtle qualities of the flowers. To strengthen the process, the person could also use affirmations, either of their own design or as suggested by a supplier of flower essences.

The Flower Essence Society has published a pioneering booklet on this theme entitled *Affirmations: The Messages of the Flowers in Transformative Words for the Soul.* As the booklet explains, "Affirmations are a specialized activity within the larger field of meditation, contemplation, and prayer. They are simple, directly evocative words which enable the soul to work toward positive, specific goals of inner development. It is a tenet of all spiritual teachings, as well as business and professional training programs, that the ordering of thought and the harmonizing of feeling has a powerful impact on our ability to manifest change, both within ourselves and within the world."

Affirmations are not magical words that immediately bring fortune or fame; rather, they are verbal tools that can help the personality to develop virtue and moral strength in accord with the real needs and capacities of the soul. Here, for example, are the FES affirmations for the three essences relating to life purpose:

Mullein

I hear the spiritual call that guides me.
I stand true to my inner guidance.
I bear aloft the torch of my Spirit Light.

Walnut

I am free of limiting influences.
I have the strength to follow inner guidance.
I break the chains that hinder my growth.

Wild Oat

I am clear in my life direction.
I express my soul's purpose in my life activities.
I create and attact the opportunities I need.

Two other flower essences that are particularly appropriate to the times we live in are iris and mountain pride. Iris was the Greek goddess of the rainbow, and the iris flower is said to create a rainbow bridge in consciousness for humans, linking Earth with Spirit. Mountain pride is a warrior flower; it builds strength and assertiveness in the face of great challenges. Together, iris and mountain pride ele-

Iris

I build a home between Earth
    and Spirit.
I work from the creative
    ground of my soul.
I nourish the world
    with my soul's rainbow light.

Figure 11. Iris

vate the parts of the soul that are capable of confronting the enormous psychic, social, economic, and environmental shadows we have created for ourselves.

To gain a sense of how these flowers may help empower people who have been stirred by the mythology of the Rainbow Warriors, consider the companion affirmations suggested by the Flower Essence Society:

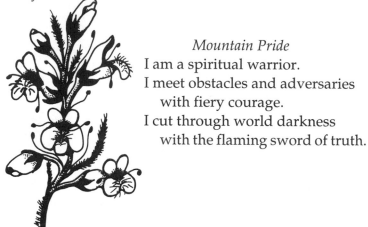

Mountain Pride
I am a spiritual warrior.
I meet obstacles and adversaries
   with fiery courage.
I cut through world darkness
   with the flaming sword of truth.

Figure 12. Mountain Pride.

Stirring words. Many people of diverse talents have a deep sense that they have a particular destiny to fulfill right now—that it is part of their life task to help the Earth in this time of transition. For them, the Age of Flowers may seem a mythic call to spiritual maturity.

For the Children

The rising hills, the slopes,
of statistics
lie before us.
the steep climb
of everything, going up,
up, as we all
go down.

In the next century
or the one beyond that,
they say,
are valleys, pastures,
we can meet there in peace
if we make it.

To climb these coming crests
one word to you, to
you and your children:

stay together
learn the flowers
go light

—Gary Snyder, *Turtle Island* (1969)
Winner of the Pulitzer Prize for
poetry, 1975

⟨⟨⟨ TEN ⟩⟩⟩

The Shambhala Vision: What It Means To Be a Spiritual Warrior

While the legend of the Rainbow Warriors is quintessentially American, it has correlations in parts of the world beyond America and Australia. One of the most striking correspondences to the rainbow myth is the Shambhala Vision, a source of inspiration to the people of Tibet for more than twelve centuries.

As reported in my earlier book, *Profiles in Wisdom: Native Elders Speak about the Earth*, Native Americans and Tibetans have an ancient and enduring connection. According to elders from both traditions, time-honored prophecies hold that one day, when the balance of the people and the world is marked with strife and confusion, Native Americans and Tibetans will come together with others and work to restore peace, harmony, and balance.

In her book *World as Lover, World as Self*, American author Joanna Macy tells the Shambhala legend as she learned it from Choegyal Rinpoche of the Tashi Jong Community in Northern India. What follows is a synopsis of the Shambhala Vision as she recounts it.

> As the Earth evolves, there will eventually come a time when all of life is threatened. Powerful political forces will rise in this time, forces that are predominantly barbarian—lacking discernment, refinement, and restraint. One power will be located in what is known today as the Western Hemisphere of the world, while the other will be located near the center of the Eurasian land

mass. Even though the two great powers will have many similarities, they will fear each other and use their wealth to develop and maintain terrible weapons that have the potential to devastate all life.

At this precarious point in history, Shambhala will begin to emerge. Shambhala will not be a place, but rather an understanding that lives in the hearts and minds of some of the people—the Shambhala warriors. These warriors will wear no uniforms and carry no flags; they will have no land base of their own. They will move, instead, on the terrain of the barbarians.

When Shambhala begins to emerge, the Shambhala warriors will have to live with exalted physical and moral courage, for their task will be to enter the heart of the barbarian powers, to walk the corridors of power where the decisions are made, and to dismantle the thoughts and weapons of destruction. They will do this successfully because they will know that the problems and weapons have been made by the human mind, and thus they can be unmade. The Shambhala warriors will see clearly that the threat to life on Earth comes not from outer space or a remote, satanic figure, but from the very decisions and lifestyles people have chosen.

As Macy reports, Choegyal Rinpoche said the Shambhala warriors will have only two weapons to aid them in their struggle: compassion and insight. Compassion will give them the energy, the passion, and the power to take action. Insight will guide them to apply this energy with intelligence and skill.

In her first book, *Despair and Personal Power in the Nuclear Age*, Joanna Macy writes of how the overwhelming troubles in the world can cause people to shut down, become numb, and bury themselves in diversions and entertainment in an attempt to avoid sorrow. In essence, people dread confronting the feelings of despair they harbor in response to personal and world conditions. And yet, as she concludes, "At the prospect of the extinction of civilization, feelings of grief and horror are natural."

This tendency to refuse the natural experience of sorrow exacts a steep price. It impoverishes the emotional and sensory life of people and dulls the energy essential for survival and true joy. Our despair, Macy writes, must be acknowledged and worked through. Only in this way can the potent emotional currents of this very natural human response be tapped and then expressed in the world as helpful actions.

While compassion gives the Shambhala warriors energy to act, it is also risky. It can induce emotional and psychic burnout. For this reason, the spiritual warriors also need insight; in particular, they need an understanding that all of life is connected and interrelated.

As modern physicists have demonstrated, this understanding is far more than a mystical dream: it is an actual physical fact. Via the all-pervading web of what scientists call "superstrings," at a sub-microscopic level the Statue of Liberty is literally connected to the butterflies in Nebraska and everything else. Infinitesimally delicate subatomic linkages connect everything to everything else—all energy and matter. By inevitable extension, everything is part of the same continuous web of energy and matter.

Spiritual warriors who explore and honor this universal linkage recognize that life is not an eternal battle between good and some external evil. Rather, as Choegyal Rinpoche expressed it, "Good and evil run through the landscape of every human heart." Through discipline and prayer, harmful or evil impulses can be transcended.

As spiritual warriors, we learn that our actions—when undertaken with pure intent—have repercussions throughout the web of life. Even small actions such as recycling soda bottles, forgiving a transgressor, or planting an organic garden have ramifications far beyond what we are capable of knowing or measuring.

The Sacred Path of the Warrior

Some people hold the concept of the warrior to be noble, even glorious, and they revel in accounts of history's epic battles. For others, who see how much suffering has come to the world as the result of aggression and battle, the concept of the warrior is repugnant. Clearly, the concept is in need of a redefinition that people can agree upon. As a preface for this redefinition, consider the foundation of the matter: a warrior's true and ultimate responsibility is to protect family and, by extension, all people. How can this best be done?

As understood in the Legend of the Rainbow Warriors and in the Shambhala Vision, spiritual warriors do no harm, inflict no pain, and cause no suffering. They work to set things right by good example.

In a time when many people are storing up knives, guns, and bullets to defend against the gathering clouds of a fearful future, spiritual warriors take a different tack. Warriorship for them in no way entails aggression on others; rather, it means having integrity, being brave, and standing forthrightly but peacefully for all that supports life. Their war is for safety, sanity, and respect.

The late, controversial Tibetan rinpoche, Chögyam Trungpa (1940-1987), lived and worked in North America for many years. In his remarkable book, *Shambhala: The Sacred Path of the Warrior*, he offered a series of essays on what it means to be a spiritual warrior.

Photo 17. Chögyam Trungpa Rinpoche. *Photo by Martin Janowitz from the collection of the Vajradhatu Archives.*

Trungpa wrote, "The Shambhala teachings are founded on the premise that there is basic wisdom that can help solve the world's problems. This wisdom does not belong to any one culture or religion, nor does it come only from the West or the East." Rather, it is a tradition of wisdom that has existed in many cultures at many times throughout history and has often by expressed by people, including warriors.

Based on the inspiration of Chögyam Trungpa's writings—and on the counsel of many learned elders from around the world—I offer the following insights and observations about the spiritual path.

Compendium of Wisdom Teachings

Be interested in life. As any elderly person will tell you, life passes quickly. Each of us has only a few brief cycles of time to experience and contribute to life. When you pay attention to the people and the natural world around you, boredom evaporates and you develop the capacity to experience a raw delight in being alive.

Allow yourself to be authentic. There's no need either to put on airs and boast or to denigrate yourself for what you have done or cannot do. No good will come from exaggerating your potential or ignoring your shortcomings. Release doubt and hesitation about being yourself. Relax: you are who you are. When you fear or obsess about yourself and the problems of the world, you become selfish; you build fortifications in yourself and your home so you can fend off the world. This helps not at all. When you are open and honest with yourself, you learn to be open and honest with others.

Cultivate who you are as a human being. Fully engage the truth you find in your heart. Be gentle with yourself and discover your own basic goodness. Take time to deliberately discover who you are and what you inherently have to offer. Develop compassion toward yourself so you can see your problems and your potential in perspective. Accurate and compassionate self-appraisal is essential; it creates the basis for helping yourself and then others.

Acknowledge your fears of yourself, others, and the world, and then go beyond them. Everyone experiences fear; it's a basic human condition. True bravery does not mean eliminating fear; it means confronting fear and then going beyond it.

Recognize that sadness, even deep grief, is likely to be a part of your response to world conditions. How can anyone look upon the homelessness, the pollution, and the corruption and not feel grief? To deny this grief is to repress a profoundly powerful source of energy. Only when you acknowledge the energy of grief can you find the strength to move from despair into an empowered stance toward life.

Discover that satisfaction and the real goodness of life come from appreciating simple experience. When you see the sunrise or a baby's smile, when you hear a bird sing or feel the wind upon your skin, take time to acknowledge and appreciate its beauty. This enriches your life and makes it possible for you to extend this fundamental goodness out into the world in other ways.

Find and follow your own vision. If you allow yourself to become trapped in an activity, occupation, or relationship that leaves unfulfilled the calling of your heart, you will feel frustrated and unhappy. The calling of your heart may not lead you to fame and fortune, but it will guide you to make an important contribution to the world, and it will lead to satisfaction.

Renounce barriers between yourself and others. This is the spiritual warrior's act of supreme courage. When you make yourself more available, more gentle, and more open to other people, you will find your experience to be full and exquisitely vivid. This is both your gift to life and your reward for being alive.

Consider that little is to be gained by creating an enemy and conquering him or her to make yourself feel better. Every human being has good and bad attributes. Rather than focusing solely upon what you deem as bad in the world, focus on what you can do to support what you see as good and helpful.

Foster a personal sense of thanksgiving. This concept is a primary Native American teaching. In the way of Turtle Island, people do not so much pray for things they want as they do direct their thoughts and words in gratitude for the gifts they already have: another day to live, sunshine, rain, food, flowers, friendship. When you appreciate the world, you don't make a mess in it with what you say or do.

Celebrate life. As you learn to appreciate the basic goodness of life—in warmth, human feeling, colors, and so forth—you will naturally develop a sense of upliftment. Express this in celebrations of ritual and ceremony, according to the traditions of your heart. When you sing, dance, and pray with others, you give something back to life rather than just taking. This helps to keep the balance of nature and to knit families and communities together.

Cultivate good humor. Some people, upon discovering a truth they feel the world needs, become so passionate that they are willing to kill or to die for it; they beat their ideas and themselves into others and eventually into the ground. Other people threaten to commit suicide because they aren't getting what they think they deserve out of life. Lighten up. A genuine sense of good humor means having a light touch as you deal with yourself and reach out to the world.

Respect your body as the physical home of your spirit. Entire libraries of books have been written on the themes of good nutrition, fresh air, and regular exercise; most carry worthwhile messages. As a spiritual warrior, you require a foundation of good health maintained with a diet of simple, clean food. In the same vein, respect the Earth as the physical home of humanity's collective spirit.

Avoid sloppiness in your personal appearance, home, and work. These reveal and intensify feelings of depression, hopelessness, and futility. Everything worth doing is worth doing well.

Sit and stand erectly; breathe fully and consciously. When you slouch, you cannot breath properly, which is the beginning of neurosis. Your posture is an outward expression of your soul as it mediates between heaven and Earth. Habitual slouching scrambles the flow of energy. When you sit and stand with dignity, you proclaim to yourself and to the world that you are a warrior, fully present, fully human. When you breathe fully, you engage with life fully.

Synchronize your mind and body. As Chögyam Trungpa wrote, this "is not a concept or a random technique someone thought up for self-improvement. Rather, it is a basic principle of how to be a human being, and of how to use your your mind and body together." This principle involves seeing, hearing, and feeling fully and carefully so that your responses will be based on reality, not on what you have imagined.

Tell the truth. Shed any hesitation about maintaining an attitude of fundamental honesty concerning the way things are and what is happening around you. Falsehood at any level smears the world with confusion and conflict. Only truth can clear this away. Spiritual warriors bear witness to the truth, without malice. When you tell the truth to others, you create an opportunity for them to express themselves honestly as well.

Speak gently and directly. Spiritual warriors neither bark nor whine. Firm but gentle speech expresses your inherent dignity and carries true authority.

Extend respect to the whole circle of life. If you want the respect of other people, you must respect them—even though you may not like them. True humility means recognizing that everyone you meet has something to teach you. Likewise, respect the soil, the air, the water, and all the creations—even the earthworms—that make your life possible.

Touch the Earth. For maximum physical and mental health, make contact with the Earth. When you touch your hands, bare feet, or body to the land, you establish a necessary bioelectric circuit with the blue-green planet that provides all your food, water, and shelter. This is analogous to the life-energy connection you had with your mother while you lived in her womb. By making conscious contact with the physical Earth, you bring yourself naturally and gently into harmony with it. As experience will show, touching the breast of the Earth regularly and in a sacred manner yields nurturance and stability—two foundational elements of a healthy life.

Maintain your balance in the face of either good or bad news. Exaggerated responses to success or failure, whether personal or global, will throw you off balance. The spiritual warrior seeks to be solidly rooted and to trust in his or her heart. Bad news and failures are acknowledged and examined; good news and successes are appreciated. Life goes on.

Work with your life situation as it is now. The past is over; the future is not here yet. The spiritual warrior does not divert energy by longing for additional gifts, opportunities, or resources, but works with what is at hand, step by step.

Honor the wisdom tradition of your family. You were born into a particular family and wisdom tradition for a reason. Though your parents may not have followed it, and though you may not feel called to follow it, there is something there for you to learn. Only by studying and examining your family roots and traditions can you master the lessons.

Heed the Seven Generations teaching. The Seven Generations principle is a nearly universal element of Native American culture. Before you make a major decision or take a major action, reflect: Who were your parents, grandparents, and great-grandparents, seven generations back in your ancestral lineage? Who are your children, or the children in your life? Who will their children be, and the children of those children, seven generations into the future? When you are sure that your actions and decisions will honor the past and the present, and also safeguard the future for seven generations, you may proceed in good conscience.

Honor the elders. Throughout history, every successful culture has honored its older members. Age conveys the benefit of experience, and in many cases experience leads to wisdom. By listening carefully and respectfully to what the elders say, you may benefit from the wisdom they represent. In turn, the elders will realize that their lives still have important meaning for their culture.

Regard your family and home as sacred, no matter how humble or grand. Otherwise, you create a huge gap between your vision for society and the reality of your everyday existence. The only way to implement your vision for society is to first create it within your own family and household. The appreciation of sacredness begins with taking a respectful interest in details—the cooking of food, the washing of dishes, the changing of diapers. An enlightened society rests on a foundation of enlightened families and homes.

Remember that a warrior's true job is to protect the people. Of necessity, this implies protecting your territory—the Earth—and supporting it so that it may bring forth an abundance of clean food and water. Without this, no warrior can claim to have protected the people in general, or their own family in particular.

Look beyond yourself and your home to see how you can help the world. This is a basic human responsibility, and a privilege.

Work ceaselessly to be an example of rightness in your life and career without being righteous about it. Nothing is quite so irritating to others as sanctimony and self-righteousness. What can you do to improve yourself and your work in the world?

Develop a specific set of skills. High ideas and good intentions are of little value unless they are harnessed to skills and discipline. Whether you are a teacher, a healer, a homemaker, a farmer, an environmentalist, or a builder, you must master the techniques that will allow you to do your work effectively.

Learn to see yourself as more than your job or your role in the world. Not everyone has a paid job that fulfills their heart's desire. Still, at work or outside work, you can make an important contribution. In this, quantity is far less important than quality.

Check the impulse to abuse power. Everyone develops some power as a human being and consequently has the opportunity to wield that power either positively or negatively. You can see this in relationships and careers, as well as in the arts, sciences, and government. When they seek power or a vision, the Lakota Sioux people often pray in this way: "I ask this not for myself alone, but so the people may live." A similar prayer will help you to anchor your ego so it does not get out of hand.

Avoid the temptation of imposing your ideas and philosophy on others. This is high arrogance, based upon fundamental insecurity about yourself and your view of truth. Ideological aggression only creates additional resentment and chaos in the world. Some people think the world needs capitalism, others think it needs communism or a particular religious theory like Christianity or Buddhism. But when ideas are pushed upon people, it constitutes a grievous violation of free will. If you are living a wise life, and if your ideas have merit, trust that other people will recognize this and that, of their own free will, they will support you and your efforts.

Sit in a circle. The council circle, or sacred hoop, is a time-honored way of ensuring that everyone is seen and heard, and that all the people have a chance to place their "good mind" on the question at hand. When challenges arise in your family, workplace, or community, gather in a circle with all the people who are directly concerned. In the council circle, each person speaks in turn and then listens respectfully to all others. The circle is an especially helpful form in times of great change.

Ponder first, then dare. Carefully consider the challenges before you, applying intelligence, intuition, and prayer; then act. The late American president Teddy Roosevelt put this teaching into a memorable statement: "Far better it is to dare mighty things, to win glorious triumphs, even though checkered by failure, than to take rank with those poor spirits who neither enjoy much nor suffer much, because they live in the grey twilight that knows not victory nor defeat."

Refuse to give up on anyone or anything worthwhile, including yourself. Each of us has problems, and the world itself, clearly, has great problems. Spiritual warriors recognize that steady effort brings results. We can, ultimately, build an enlightened society. But this requires great courage.

Ponder your mortality. You will die someday. What will your legacy be? How will you be remembered?

Bear in mind that wisdom is not some monumental thing outside yourself. You are related to all things, including the inherent wisdom and goodness of the universe. Spiritual warriorship is not a program or a set of techniques that you apply when an obstacle arises or when you are unhappy: it is a continual journey. To be a spiritual warrior is to be genuine every moment of your life and to take joy in the journey.

⟨⟨⟨⟨EPILOGUE⟩⟩⟩⟩

A vision without a task is a dream. A task without a vision is drudgery. But a vision with a task can change the world.
—Black Elk

*A*ll these tales and much more, this is the Legend of the Rainbow Warriors. Once again, in yet another way, the story has been told. Readers must ask, is the telling enough? Is the telling true? Did our native ancestors have an accurate vision of a New Age and of the Rainbow Warriors?

The cumulative evidence that we are in a time of profound Earth change is unmistakable. Even political leaders invoke phrases such as New World Order, though they give scant definition of what they mean when they use such words. By any estimation, planetary upheaval surrounds us on all fronts. Many thousands of people have joined their efforts and resources on behalf of the Earth, whether they think of themselves as Rainbow Warriors or not. But does any of this make the myth real?

I make no special claim of ultimate truth for the perspective shared in this book. The voices, both ancient and modern, are authentic; the current affairs are accurate and verifiable from standard references. But how, in the end, shall the reader put them together?

While I will venture no bold claim of ultimate truth for the conclusions suggested in this book, I will say this: they are part of my truth. I offer the legend of the Rainbow Warriors in the hope that it will raise helpful questions for you, the reader: What is your myth? What gives your life its meaning? How are you acting to make your myth a living part of the world's experience? If the Legend of the Rainbow Warriors speaks to you, what can you do to make this myth real, to engage more directly in the ancient quest of heroes and heroines: bringing heaven to Earth?

Today, as ever, we face the present and the future. According to the mythology of Harmonic Convergence, we are in a critical twenty-five-year epoch of change—change that is more far-reaching and enigmatic than at any other time in history. The necessity for taking meaningful action is therefore not ten years away, or even next year, but now. The event known as Harmonic Convergence can, in a certain light, be understood as the start of a time when every human being is called to awaken as a Rainbow Warrior—someone who lives in support of, and with respect for, all of the creations on Earth.

As documented in this book, the world events that occurred in apparent connection with Harmonic Convergence are rapidly changing our worldview. We can see ever more clearly that our planet is but a mote of dust in a vast universe—and that we have much more to learn about ourselves and the spiral of our neighborhood galaxy, the Milky Way. As we recognize this connection more distinctly through science and expanding spiritual perception, we can grasp more fully that we are part of a vast, ordered universe.

Cherokee and Buddhist teacher Dhyani Ywahoo puts it this way: "We are moving around the spiral, coming again to a place of whole civilization, of true planetary consciousness. What we see now are the fever throes, the end of the fever's nightmares as the sickness and poisons leave the system. It is a mistake to focus on the fever; instead, we need to focus on the means of healing."

One powerful modern myth has been formed by the advertising industry with its images of vast, luxurious wealth; another has been formed by the bloody horror movies that dominate VCR tape sales and rentals. For many thousands of people, in the absence of something more wholesome, such barren and chaotic visions have become their personal working myths. The Legend of the Rainbow Warriors offers an alternative of hope and happy possibility based upon personal responsibility.

The New World Order we hear politicians speak of seems, to many, vaguely ominous. Perhaps this is because, lacking clear definition, the New World Order seems to consist of vast, impersonal government bureaucracies, interlocking and unknowable financial networks, multinational corporations with allegiance only to profit, the loss of personal privacy, and the advance of sophisticated technologies without regard to their consequences. We cannot help but wonder about the places of the individual and the family in this context.

Likewise, many people, particularly from fundamentalist traditions, have been fearful of the alternative myths of the New Age and the rainbow. They sense in these myths a threat to what they hold sacred. As someone who has explored and reported on these myths for nearly twenty years, I have also, on occasion, seen cause for concern: individuals and groups headed in what I take as manipulative or impractical directions. But these have been the exceptions. Most of what I have seen has been wholesome, respectful, and empowering. What might be called the New Age movement is not ultimately about crystals or channeling. It has no central leader or organization; control and hierarchy, in fact, are the antithesis of this emerging myth. Rather, this movement is about individual freedom and responsibility for self, family, community, and planet—and the recognition that all these elements are inextricably connected.

Folksinger Bob Dylan put it well many years ago when, with irony, he sang, "Don't follow leaders, watch your parking meters." The Rainbow movement, to the extent that it is a movement, is as decentralized and diverse as the human community; it's about people following their personal visions and offering the gift of their visions to the larger community of life on the planet. Whether they think of themselves as Christian, Buddhist, Jewish, Native American, or something else, Rainbow Warriors recognize the fundamental necessity of respecting differences and honoring the Earth we all share together.

No doubt some of you will regard the *Legend of the Rainbow Warriors* as a grade B fantasy and scoff at the notion that there is any credible verification for such a hopeful and holistic worldview. To you I say, "Study the texts of science. Read what the leading physicists, mathematicians, and biologists are saying now about the nature of reality and the fundamental fact of our connectedness.

Study the revelations of quantum mechanics, relativity, chaos theory, and superstrings."

There is far more evidence to support the emerging holistic philosophies of a New Age than there is to buttress the widely held belief that we are separate from other aspects of creation and that we live our lives as individuals, unaffected by dreams, untouched by mystery. In the seeming contrast of these worldviews, there is paradox—paradox that may well occupy forward-thinking people for generations to come.

As I understand the myth, the Rainbow Warriors are not likely to come charging onto the scene like the cavalry to save us, nor should we hold our breath waiting for them to arrive en masse from parts unknown. The Rainbow Warriors are here already, and we are they. That is, we are if we choose to be, no matter the color of our skin or the name of our religion. Out of our diversity, we find strength and unity. This is an essential part of the Legend of the Rainbow Warriors: the understanding that every facet and shade of the rainbow is necessary for its integrity and beauty.

In North America, we have long cherished the myth of the melting pot. Out of the many diverse cultures streaming onto this continent and weaving themselves together, one new race of people would ultimately emerge. Might not that melting pot be the one at the end of the rainbow?

The future will be whatever we make of it. What myth will we follow? What dream will we pursue for ourselves, our children, and our grandchildren unto seven generations? These are the questions we must answer as we move to, and then beyond, the millennium.

If you count yourself among the Rainbow Warriors, then realize that you may not always be called to glorious tasks before the public eye. The rainbow bridge to a new world is built each day through hard work and the seemingly small decisions we all make. Can you find a nonpolluting detergent for washing your clothes? Can you install a solar water heater? Can you plant an organic garden or support a local farmer? Will you treat the plants and animals with respect? Will you remember the Earth as you make your nightly prayers? Can you help your family, neighbors, or community to grow in some way? With such small, steady steps as these is myth made real.

If the myth of Daedalus can come to life as a human being spreads synthetic wings and flies over the sea using only the strength of his body for power, and if the myth of space travel can propel humans to walk on the moon, then the Legend of the Rainbow Warriors and the myth of a New Age can also become real. This much is certain. We can, if we choose, build a world that works for everyone.

⟨⟨⟨⟨ GENERAL RESOURCES ⟩⟩⟩⟩

Sun Bear*
Bear Tribe Medicine Society
P.O. Box 9167
Spokane, WA 99209

Greenpeace
P.O. Box 96099
Washington, DC 20090-6099

Scott Guynup
Illustrator, Visionary Artist
707 Brunswick Drive
Waynesville, NC 28786

Brooke Medicine Eagle
Sky Lodge
P.O. Box 121
Ovando, MT 59854

Medicine Story (Manitonquat)
Mettanokit Community
c/o Another Place
Route 123
Greenville, NH 03048

Hunbatz Men
Communidad Indigena Maya
APDO Postal 7-013
Merida 7
Yucatán, Mexico

Twylah Nitsch
Wolf Clan Teaching Lodge
12199 Brant Reservation Road
Brant, NY 14027-0136

Shambhala Warrior Training
2130 Arapaho
Boulder, CO 80302

Oh Shinnah
Four Directions Foundation
P.O. Box 56-1685
Miami, FL 33256-1685

Dhyani Ywahoo
Sunray Meditation Society
P.O. Box 308
Bristol, VT 05443

*Before he passed away, Sun Bear asked the members of the Bear Tribe Medicine Society to carry on his activities and teachings.

⟪⟪⟪ FLORAL RESOURCES ⟫⟫⟫

Alaskan Flower Essence Project
1153 Donna Drive
Fairbanks, AK 99712
(907) 457-2440

Australian Bush Flower Essences
Box 351
Spit Junction, NSW
Australia 2088

Australian Flower Essence Academy
P.O. Box 355, Scarborough 6019
Perth, Australia
(09) 244-2073
Fax: (09) 244-2072

Aveda (flower-based shampoos)
400 Pheasant Ridge Drive
Blaine, MN 55434
800-328-0849

Bach Flower Remedies
Bach/Ellon Company
Box 320
Woodmere, NY 11598

Flower Essence Society
P.O. Box 459
Nevada City, CA 95959
800-548-0075
Fax: (916) 265-6467

Ozark Flower Essences
HCR 73, Box 160
Drury, MO 65638
(417) 679-3391

Pacific Institute of Aromatherapy
P.O. Box 606
San Rafael, CA 94915
(415) 924-3390

Pegasus Products, Inc.
P.O. Box 228
Boulder, CO 80306
(303) 442-0139

Perelandra, Ltd.
Box 136
Jeffersonton, VA 22724

Vita Florum, Ltd.
Coombe Castle Elworthy
Taunton, Somerset
England TA4 3PX

Vita Florum, Inc.
c/o Satyena Ananda
Starseed
Chapel Rd.
Savoy, MA 01256

⟨⟨⟨ BIBLIOGRAPHY ⟩⟩⟩

Argüelles, José. *Mayan Factor: Path Beyond Technology.* Santa Fe, NM: Bear & Company, 1987.

Balin, Peter. *The Flight of the Feathered Serpent.* Wilmot, WI: Arcana Publishing Co., 1978.

Boissière, Robert. *The Return of Pahana: A Hopi Myth.* Santa Fe, NM: Bear & Company, 1990.

Book of J. Translated from the Hebrew by David Rosenberg and interpreted by Harold Bloom. New York: Vintage Books, 1991.

Brown, Dee. *Bury My Heart at Wounded Knee.* New York: Washington Square Press, 1970.

Brown, Joseph Epes. *The Sacred Pipe: Black Elk's Account of the Seven Rites of the Oglala Sioux.* Middlesex, England: Penguin Books, 1953.

Brown, Michael, and John May. *The Greenpeace Story.* London: Dorling Kindersley, Ltd., 1989.

Brown, Vinson. *Voices of Earth and Sky: The Vision Life of the Native Americans.* Happy Camp, CA: Naturegraph Publishers, Inc., 1974.

Buenfil, Alberto Ruz. *Rainbow Nation Without Borders: Toward an Ecotopian Millennium.* Santa Fe, NM: Bear & Company, 1991.

Campbell, Joseph. *The Hero with a Thousand Faces.* Princeton, NJ: Princeton University Press, 1956.

_____. *Myths to Live By.* New York: Viking Books, 1972.

Chinmoy, Sri. *Kundalini: The Mother-Power.* Jamaica, NY: Aum Publications, 1974.

Davidson, Gordon, and Corrine McLaughlin. *The Spiritual Heritage and Destiny of the United States.* New York: Prentice-Hall, 1991.

Fox, Matthew. *Original Blessing.* Santa Fe, NM: Bear & Company, 1983.

Iron Thunderhorse and Donn Le Vie, Jr. *Return of the Thunderbeings.* Santa Fe, NM: Bear & Company, 1990.

Kaiser, Rudolf. *The Voice of the Great Spirit: Prophecies of the Hopi Indians.* Boston, MA: Shambhala Publications, Inc., 1991.

Kaminski, Patricia, and Richard Katz. *Affirmations: The Messages of the Flowers in Transformative Words for the Soul.* Nevada City, CA: Flower Essence Society, 1989.

Macy, Joanna. *Despair and Personal Power in the Nuclear Age.* Philadelphia, PA: New Society Publishing, 1983.

_____. *World as Lover, World as Self.* Berkeley, CA: Parallax Press, 1991.

McFadden, Steven. *Profiles in Wisdom: Native Elders Speak about the Earth.* Santa Fe, NM: Bear & Company, 1991.

Men, Hunbatz. *Secrets of Mayan Science/Religion.* Santa Fe, NM: Bear & Company, 1990.

Needleman, Jacob. *The Way of the Physician.* New York: Harper & Row, 1985.

Neihardt, John G. *Black Elk Speaks.* New York: William Morrow and Co., 1932.

Peterson, Scott. *Native American Prophecies.* New York: Paragon House, 1990.

Robbins, Tom. *Jitterbug Perfume.* New York: Bantam Books, 1984.

Schaff, Gregory. *Wampum Belts and Peace Trees: George Morgan, Native Americans and Revolutionary Diplomacy.* Golden, CO: Fulcrum Publishing, 1990.

Shearer, Tony. *Beneath the Moon and Under the Sun: A Reappraisal of the Sacred Calendar and the Prophecies of Ancient Mexico.* Santa Fe, NM: Sun Publishing Co., 1975.

_____. *Lord of the Dawn, Quetzalcoatl: Great Prophecies of Ancient Mexico.* Happy Camp, CA: Naturegraph Publishers, Inc., 1971.

Snyder, Gary. *Turtle Island.* New York: New Directions Books, 1969.

Sun Bear and Wabun Wind, *Black Dawn, Bright Day.* Spokane, WA: Bear Tribe Publishing, 1990.

Thompson, William Irwin. *Blue Jade from the Morning Star: An Essay and A Cycle of Poems on Quetzalcoatl.* West Stockbridge, MA: The Lindisfarne Press, 1983.

Trungpa, Chögyam. *Shambhala: The Sacred Path of the Warrior.* Boston, MA: Shambhala Publications, 1984.

Waters, Frank. *The Book of the Hopi.* Middlesex, England: Penguin Books, 1963.

Willoya, William, and Vinson Brown. *Warriors of the Rainbow: Strange and Prophetic Dreams of the Indian Peoples.* Happy Camp, CA: Naturegraph Publishers, 1962.

Ywahoo, Dhyani. *Voices of Our Ancestors: Cherokee Teachings from the Wisdom Fire.* Boston, MA: Shambhala Publications, Inc., 1987.

⸨⸨⸨ ABOUT THE AUTHOR ⸩⸩⸩

*S*teven McFadden writes, counsels, and gardens from his home in rural New Hampshire. A journalist, a farm activist, and an astrologer, Steven is also a master in the traditional Reiki system of healing. As director for the Planetary Wisdom Keepers project, he has been meeting with learned elders from around the world for a forthcoming book and video series.

Steven is the author of *Profiles in Wisdom: Native Elders Speak About the Earth* (1991) and coauthor with Trauger Groh of *Farms of Tomorrow: Community Supported Farms, Farm Supported Communities* (1990). He is also a contributing writer to *Ecologue: The Environmental Catalogue and Consumer's Guide for a Safe Earth* (1990).

Steven has worked with groups in both corporate and private settings since 1975, and he travels widely to offer lectures and workshops. You may contact him at:

Chiron Communications
P.O. Box 481
New Ipswich, NH 03071

BOOKS OF RELATED INTEREST
BY BEAR & COMPANY

CRYING FOR A DREAM
The World Through Native American Eyes
by Richard Erdoes

GIFT OF POWER
The Life and Teachings of a Lakota Medicine Man
by Archie Fire Lame Deer and Richard Erdoes

THE MAYAN FACTOR
Path Beyond Technology
by José Argüelles

THE PRAYING FLUTE
Song of the Earth Mother
by Tony Shearer

PROFILES IN WISDOM
Native Elders Speak about the Earth
by Steven McFadden

RAINBOW NATION WITHOUT BORDERS
Toward an Ecotopian Millennium
by Alberto Ruz Buenfil

SACRED PLACES
How the Living Earth Seeks Our Friendship
by James Swan

Contact your local bookseller or write:
BEAR & COMPANY
P.O. Drawer 2860
Santa Fe, NM 87504